To Shane,

Your friendship, this last season of my life means more than you know brother! I deeply value your wisdom, grace, patience, and your heart of a peacemaker.

Every time you read this story, may it stir a fire in your soul, that through Jesus, no matter what you face, you can forever...

RISE TO ALIVE !!

Kevin

John 14:6

TESTIMONIALS

"I have been working on the African mission field since 2011, which has blessed me with the encounter of many miraculous healings. While these encounters have produced a hopeful, expectant heart in the face of tragedies, I rarely have carried that faith off the continent with me. *RISE! Miracle Through a Father's Eyes* is the perfect reminder that we should expect God to meet us in every tragedy we encounter through life, and we should expect the miraculous! Things don't always go as we expect, life can change in the blink of an eye, and in our darkest times, it truly can be difficult to have hope. In this book, Kevin Clayton truly models the faith, love, and perseverance God has called us to on this side of eternity."

—Erik Laursen, M. Phil.,
President & CEO of New Covenant Missions

"You simply must take the time to read this book. This heartfelt and extremely well-written true chronicle will activate your faith and implore you to believe once again in miracles. In times of darkness, we need the inspiring light that burns within these pages."

—Zach Bryant,
educator and lifelong friend to the author

TESTIMONIALS (continued)

"*RISE! Miracle Through a Father's Eyes* is intensely genuine, transparent, and bold in a time when these qualities are loosely held though they should be greatly treasured. This book will challenge you to acknowledge death *without* identifying with it or letting it overcome you. Having been there for all the major events of my nephew Mark Clayton's life—including the day he was born, the day he graduated high school, and the day he was married—I am thankful to have witnessed the epic battle and victory that took place in these pages as well. I fully believe and pray *RISE!* will help challenge and motivate you to live each day in the fullness of life and overcome death even in the hardest of all our trials and suffering."

—Chris Clayton,
brother to the author

"This is a story about a miracle, a true story. Whether you believe in miracles or not—too late—it already happened. I was there. Having been honored to walk in friendship with the Clayton family for over two decades, I have witnessed what it means to be part of this tribe. Love, and love hard. Believe, and never give up—even when it looks like all is lost. This book is a vulnerable and painfully honest telling of loss, grief, and resurrection—the journey of a father warring for his son's life and his own faith. In an age where true fatherhood has gone by the wayside, Kevin's fiery and unshakable love for his family is a timely testament to the *LOVE* of the fiery and unshakable God. Not only did it invigorate (again) my faith in a miracle-working God, but it pointed me straight into the love of the Father. You will get lost in these pages, and if you're willing, find a faith of your own worth fighting for!"

—Spirit Laursen,
longtime friend to the author

RISE!
Miracle Through
a Father's Eyes

Kevin Clayton

RISE!
Miracle Through
a Father's Eyes

www.risetoalive.com

All quotations and sources referenced in Notes.

Copyright © 2022 by Kevin S. Clayton

Published in the United States of America.

1st Printing

First Edition

Edited by select committee.
Special thanks to all who contributed to this effort!

Graphic Cover & Interior Book Design by Kevin Clayton

DEDICATION

To Crystal... my beautiful blue-eyed angel, a treasure—There are no words to express how much you mean to me. Not a single page of this book would be possible if you had not come into my life; I would not have the soul mate that I have already shared over a quarter of a century with, nor the two incredible sons that you birthed which we have loved so deeply since they entered this world. Our life together has been overflowing with laughter and sorrow, joy and pain, highs and lows, faith and fear, love and loss, all of which created a fathomless bond I never imagined possible when I first met you. The miracles we have encountered together, none more than the one which is the subject of this book, continue to impact us to the core of our beings and forever change us. My love, you are a treasure to me in this world and the next, a rare gem with a value that only myself and our Creator will ever truly know. I could not have survived this chapter of our story (or any for that matter) without your grace, strength, and love!

To Mark... my oldest son, a miracle—From the first moment we locked eyes when you were a newborn, I knew that you were extraordinary and unique. I used to joke when you were little that you were indestructible, but I had no idea how you would test that idea and have it remain true throughout your years of life to this point! I love your energy, your humor, and your heart of a lion. To be a father has been one of the greatest gifts in this world, and I have learned more about life and God through you than you will ever know. I am a stronger, richer, and more resilient man because of you; for that, I am forever grateful, as I experience love in its purest form because you are my son.

DEDICATION (continued)

To Brian... my youngest son, a blessing—When you came into this world, I knew my life was different. There was a peace that you brought to both my heart and my reality as I lived each day. Almost losing you at such an early age awoke my soul to the fathomless love a father holds within. The moments I have had with you where I learned to be still and listen more intently to God and all the beauty that life whispers are priceless to me. I love your steadfast spirit, timely one-liners that are both funny and educational, and your quiet yet tenacious soul of a tiger. I am a deeper, fuller, and more balanced man because of you; for that, I am forever thankful, as I experience love in its truest form because you are my son.

To Bob & Cathye... my parents, a pair of pillars—I had no idea what the two of you offered, sacrificed, and fought for until I became a parent myself. As a man, I am honored to continue to watch the two of you strive after the heart of God. As your son, I am thankful beyond measure for what you have sown into me over the years and your incredible support in bringing this book into being.

To Family & Friends... I would never have been able to become the man I am today without your encouragement, challenges, laughter, empathy, acceptance, grace, and wisdom. However, we are not finished. May we find new ways to rise in our relationships until we cross over into the afterlife—a new world free of pain or suffering and full of infinite goodness. I love you all more than you know and pray that each of you will choose every day, an authentic deep relationship with me and others for the rest of your life! There is more, so much more; we need only to seek it out and then rise to live it.

DEDICATION (continued)

To Jesus... I met you at the influenceable age of 16, and you transformed me. I started then a journey of getting to know you. I was now in the presence of a King, yet You knew me and related to me not merely as Your "subject," but as Your child whom You loved. You joined me where I *was*, young and immature, to begin teaching me, disciplining me, revealing truths to me, loving me in and through my brokenness, and healing me from the pains brought upon me by myself and others. Ironically though, I had no clue how powerful You were, how mighty You *are*! I had read the stories about You and listened to others speak of You, but now I knew You for myself. How naïve I have been for so many years of my life—how accidentally irreverent I was of You as a Savior, for me and everyone on the face of this planet. I look back on the road traveled to this point of my life and can only be humbled as well as utterly awe-struck at Your greatness. After living the phenomenon of the storied pages herein, I am no longer naïve to Your power, mercy, grace, and love. I can only thank You—for being faithful during my failings, for Your patience as I attempt to persevere, and for Your salvation despite my skepticism. I trust You and will remain in Your debt every moment of the rest of my life for illuminating me to Your power even over death itself. May I live each day to rise in this—Your absolute sovereignty.

CONTENTS

INTRODUCTION

Life after death is an ideological, philosophical, and theological space that has been explored, debated, and feared since the dawn of the human being. It is the grand finale of our living, to utter our last breath and cross over into the afterlife. What happens, however, when we are confronted with a death that is not our *own* physical expiration from this earth but someone else's? Furthermore, what happens when death unexpectedly appears outside the physical realm to threaten our goals, dreams, finances, relationships, and whole perspective on life itself? Death is not merely a *physical* force; it can and will steal life from us *emotionally* and *spiritually* while we still live!

I encountered death for the first time as a young boy, just 10 years old, when my grandfather, my dad's father, passed away from failing health. He had spent years working in a printing press while dipping his hands directly in ink, among other hazards which eventually ruined his internal organs. Being both fortunate and cursed with a photographic memory, I am blessed and burdened with permanent snapshots that lodge themselves in my mind as I live this life every day.

One of the earliest mind photographs I can remember is standing in front of my grandfather's open casket at his funeral while I stared at his lifeless face as my grandmother held his hand while crying. It was the first encounter I had with death, the first scar it put on me, but it would not be the last.

Wow, these first two paragraphs are heavy and sad, so I am not sure I want to read on you say? I understand. Death is a

INTRODUCTION

depressing reality, not something we want to think about for even a moment, much less face with any regularity in our existence. Make no mistake, though; death is inevitable—how we feel about it, whatever our experience has been with it, we cannot escape it. We all have, or certainly will, face the death of a family member, friend, or acquaintance at some point during the timeline of our life. Moreover, we have all felt the sting of a dream dying, a job terminated, a relationship perishing—all things we do not usually equate to being synonymous with death.

> **Death is not merely a *physical* force; it can and will steal life from us *emotionally* and *spiritually* while we still live.**

In my experience, the willful avoidance or blatant denial of discussing death in all its forms only feeds the fear of it whilst extinguishing any encounter we might have within the *entire* experience. The entirety is the truth—the good news—that death is *not* the end. Hear me clearly; there *is* life after death. For this reason, you should want to read on. You do not want to miss the story herein, as it is not about death; it is about what happens *beyond* death—it is the realization of what transpires when we *RISE*!

Nature provides beautiful examples of life after death. There is one illustration I have always loved. I first heard it in simple form within a message delivered by a summer camp speaker when I was young, which painted a picture that thoroughly resonated with me. It is an image I continue to return to regularly to help me digest the pain and wreckage that life has wrought upon me at one time or another. In my own words, I will repaint

INTRODUCTION

the illustration spoken to me long ago for you in the next paragraph below, hoping that you may enjoy this vision in the context of your life for years to come.

Imagine a wildfire burning out of control, flames as tall as buildings moving at speeds making it nigh unto impossible to escape; walls of heat driven it seems by the very breath of hell, producing massive pillars of life choking smoke. Without remorse or mercy, it brutally imposes itself on every living thing in its path, viciously ravaging this forest, leaving nothing but the black char of death and the stench of lifeless silence. To survey such devastation, one would guess that no living thing would be able to inhabit such a wasteland ever again. Yet, just days after this utter annihilation, new life begins to spring forth out of the ashes, replacing savage soot with colorful creation. Give it time; what once was a charcoal wilderness covered in dark decomposition with merely faint memoirs of the living upon it will flourish in stunning color and beauty, with luminous life overpowering all the dismal decay.

This image-laden landscape of life after death is the perfect foundational analogy for what will follow in pages turned. It takes courage to look death in the face—yet one can do so with eager anticipation of what awaits afar—past the edges of the map, beyond what we expect to navigate as "normal" human beings.

Regardless of your background or what you have experienced in life to this point, irrespective of what you have believed in the past or think you might believe in the future, regardless of your position on religion or spirituality, there simply are those rare occurrences when life defies death to the antithesis of all conventional human logic. These anomalies baffle our beliefs, rebel against reason, evade typical explanations, provoke passion, and challenge every core conviction.

So right here, right now, I want to invite you into something that took place in the sunny state of South Carolina, but more importantly, something that took place at the uncommon crossroad where raw humanity meets perceptible spirituality. What happened at that crossroad ignited a fuse, which once lit burned quickly to a detonation of physical, emotional, and spiritual napalm—which then explosively moved through the head, heart, hospital, counties, states, and even across oceans to other continents.

Rarely does one happen upon such a crossroad, much less get to be involved first-hand. So, I would be completely remiss if I did not want to share what happened in my life as well as the lives of my family and friends on one fateful day as well as the arduous and miraculous days after.

It would be easy to treat this like any other novel, a fantastic fictional tale that we have read on so many other different pages throughout our lives. Perhaps you have already started skimming the words of this introduction unconsciously, or even consciously for whatever reason, thinking that nothing substantial ever is said in the rambling preamble of a book. STOP. *PLEASE.*

I implore you to pause the typical procedure and protocol of pragmatic thinking right now in favor of a *conscious* choice to chance the cracked door in front of you and accept an invitation into a world beyond. This very instant, take captive your active psyche and commit to going on this journey, seeing it through amenably to the very last word.

Leave behind preconceived notions, plagiarized stereotypes, and passive or aggressive condemnations. Shed your conscious or unconscious skepticism and your inklings of insecurities. Chain up your every carnal nature that would disregard, dismiss, or diminish anything that you are about to read. Why? Because I believe with every bit of my being that a transformational thesis, as well as a full glimpse into eternity, lies herein.

To fully reach such potent powers, however, there must be a genuine candor—authentic transparency in narration. As such, I commit the following to you as a reader who dared open the pages of this modern-day scroll; I am painfully reliving, openly revealing, and expectantly retelling this anecdote through a father's eyes. I do this to allow you the opportunity to walk with me through one of the most terrible yet equally incredible experiences of my life. I humbly ask for your audience; I respectfully invite your interest as I pull back the curtain and let you into this profoundly personal, sincerely soulful encounter with death, life, and a realm unseen.

Without death, one cannot be witness to the implausible miracle of resurrection.

If you earnestly immerse yourself, at the very least, you may unearth a gem about yourself, others, or life that you might never have encountered before. I can only hope that you are willing to brave the pages ahead boldly and perhaps even allow my pain to penetrate your own soul—to encompass the entirety of the miracle that ensues.

It is only natural to desire evading death every time it devilishly demonstrates itself. Then again, without death, one cannot be witness to the implausible miracle of resurrection.

CHAPTER I
FATEFUL FALLING

History is a story written by the finger of God.

—C.S. Lewis

Story. Each of us is a unique story, as every chapter in our living book chronicles our time here on earth. Every event and memory, each person and place, all words and actions are etched forever onto the pages of our life's tale. For that reason alone, we should approach our existence with sincerity—to cherish every moment our heart beats and our lungs breathe.

Life is deeply replete with mystery, ecstasy, tragedy, epiphany, and dichotomy. We inevitably are encircled by all these experiences as we move through the journey of being alive. However, the most intimate revelations come in *consciously embracing* each encounter as it happens. Our direct engagement in these encounters truly allows us to be whole—to be absolutely alive.

On the other hand, death is predominantly viewed as a finality, an inevitable event from which there is no return. Hence, we spend far too much time throughout our lives with attitudes of either rebellion or fear towards death.

The adrenaline junkie jumps out of planes, mingles with wild beasts, and scales sheer cliffs, all attempting to "cheat" death and conjure up a connection with still being alive. Conversely, the fearful person avoids all dangerous hobbies and shuts themself inside unhealthily while shunning anything that may increase the risk of hurt, sickness, injury, or death. I venture to dare that there is a third life perspective; that of the *balanced* human being.

To achieve balance, we must make every effort to equalize ourselves in the middle of this pendulum of life—we need to actively strain against a violent swing from side to side as life imposes its extremes upon us. However, the hard part is we never know when such a force will rock our pendulum, creating an imbalance when we are pushed from the middle out toward the edge.

> **Life is deeply replete with mystery, ecstasy, tragedy, epiphany, and dichotomy. The most intimate revelations come in *consciously embracing* each encounter as it happens.**

When fall arrives each year for our family, Sunday is about football, food, fun, relationship, and most importantly, faith. It is a day (Sabbath) designed by God himself for rest, reflection, and the reenergizing of one's spirit for the days in the week ahead. Sunday, November 10th, 2019, started like any other Sunday, but I could never have known that this would become an unforgettable entry in this chapter of my life as well as the lives of my family and friends.

My wife Crystal, my son Brian, and I were sitting in our living room talking about the week to come, watching a little football while getting ready to wind down the evening, when

Fateful Falling

Crystal's cell phone rang a little after 8:00 p.m. (EST). The call was from Sam Wilder, whom we knew going back to when we arrived in South Carolina in 2016, as he and my sons Mark and Brian played varsity basketball together at Eastside High School during Mark and Sam's Senior year. Throughout those years, we became close friends with Sam, and his parents, Mike and Andrea.

Crystal looked down at her phone and saw the call was from Sam, so she playfully answered (as usual), expecting that if he was calling, it had to be because Mark had pulled a prank or done something hilarious. That would have been entirely normal for our comedic son, so she anticipated that Sam probably just wanted to relay the funny story himself.

The look on her face, though, quickly turned from playful to absolute horror as Sam struggled on the other end of the line to force out the words that Mark, our first-born son at just 21 years old, had collapsed outside the gym where he had gone to play basketball and was totally unresponsive.

That is the phone call that no parent ever wants to receive—that no parent should ever *have* to receive! Crystal screamed out to me the news of what was happening, "Mark collapsed, and he's unresponsive!"

Instantly it felt as if someone had pulled the pin from a live grenade and dropped it right in the center of our living room. Time totally blew up and stopped.

My ears rang, my mind spun, my heart sank, and my soul stalled. Is this real? Can this be happening?! We had just spoken to him hours before, and he was so alive, so excited to play hoops with his buddies. After that jarring detonation of dreadful news, my wife and I blasted off our recliners, rushing to make our way to that fateful church gym in Greer, SC.

RISE! MIRACLE THROUGH A FATHER'S EYES

I cleared our stairs, going up to the second level of our home in just three large lunges. I threw on jeans and a t-shirt, grabbed my wallet, truck keys, and cell phone then bolted back toward the stairs. I jumped down to the center landing in one leap from the top. Then, as I turned down the second set of stairs toward the front door, I remember looking up as the incomprehension inside me was now wholly colliding with the unfolding reality outside of me and saying aloud, "Jesus, please don't take my son?!"

It was a phrase expressed both as a question and exclamation. A question humbly directed to a God above whom I knew could save his life, as well as a desperate exclamation from an already heartbroken father unable to imagine living life without his son while demanding at the same time this *not* be the final page of his young story!

After those words rose out of my lungs and over my pursed lips, something swelled within, gripping the deepest parts of my being, though I had neither the time nor the capacity to pursue its meaning right then. I pushed it aside abruptly to focus and slammed on my shoes at the bottom of the stairs. I listened as Brian finished relaying the ominous message to Hannah, Mark's wife whom he had married only four months earlier, then we surged through the garage door, sprung into my truck, and took off in a loud blaze down our street toward Greer and our son.

As we drove that curvy two-lane country road, my wife's sorrow erupted, escalating quickly. There are few things more heart-wrenching in this world than the sound of a mother grieving over her child—it is sonorous anguish that explodes through the ears and suffocates the soul. It was truly terrible.

She cried so hard, wailing uncontrollably, as I held her hand tightly, trying to console her. Keeping her calm was no easy task, impossible in actuality, yet I felt complete empathy for her as I could feel her heart breaking just by holding her hand and hearing her weep; it was breaking *my* heart.

> **There are few things more heart-wrenching in this world than the sound of a mother grieving over her child—it is sonorous anguish that explodes through the ears and suffocates the soul.**

I burst into prayer multiple times as I drove, in between lashing out at traffic lights while perhaps carefully "bending" a few traffic laws, begging God for mercy as our winding travel drew us closer to where our son lay unconscious. It was so paralyzing, so surreal.

A flood of images and memories from my son's infancy to his 21st birthday popped like fireworks in my head, each lingering as if it had happened only yesterday. Apprehension pumped violently through my whole body. All I wanted was to be with my son, to know he was going to live, to get assurance that I would have future father-to-son encounters in this world without waiting until the afterlife.

As we came up over the bridge heading into Greer and turned the corner toward the parking lot where our son had collapsed, I saw the flashing lights and heard a siren that seemed to shriek louder directly at me than any I had ever heard before. An ambulance raced passed us on the left, and I knew it carried Mark. We did not know where he was being transported, so I rushed my truck to the curb, slammed on the brakes, and jumped out.

RISE! MIRACLE THROUGH A FATHER'S EYES

I ran directly to the EMT to get the story of what had happened and find out where the ambulance was going. I will never forget the look on his face as I came rushing up to him. He raised both hands because he could see the panic and worry on my face—but the grave reality that I read immediately, which hid behind his professional mask, struck my heart like a sledgehammer. His eyes tried hard to hide it, yet leaked the harsh truth; he did not believe my son would survive.

He calmly yet somberly relayed the facts that our son had come out of the gym to get something from his car and then collapsed a few feet from the door. He suffered two cardiac arrests and sustained multiple head and bodily injuries from falling. As if that was not already more than we could handle, he finished by saying Mark had been unresponsive for what he estimated at up to 15 minutes.

He completed his brief choppy summary by telling me Sam (Wilder) had performed chest compressions on his friend until the EMT team arrived. Once they took over, they had to hit him with the defibrillator but got a heartbeat back in my son. He informed us that Mark was on his way to Greenville Memorial Hospital, then implored us to drive safely, as we were already dashing back to our truck to chase after our son.

As we tore out of the church parking lot, my thoughts were singularly drawn to the harsh fact that if my son had been oxygen deprived for up to 15 minutes, his chance of survival was likely *zero*. I knew that, medically speaking, after 6 to 7 minutes without oxygen, survival rates drop to less than 10%. Mark may have doubled that number, so it did not bode well.

Even if he did physically survive, what brain damage might he have suffered? Would he be completely brain dead? Would he be able to return to any part of his life as it was before he collapsed? I could feel my heart cracking under the weight of it all, and suddenly I was confronted with the crisis that we all face at one point or another in life—what do I really believe about God?

> **No parent should have to bury their child; it is one of the cruelest agonies this broken world can inflict.**

It is easy to believe in a benevolent and loving God when one is receiving blessings and prosperity, but not so much when your first-born child is seemingly being ripped from your arms and life itself far too soon. No parent should have to bury their child; it is one of the cruelest agonies this broken world can inflict, and here I was faced with that harshly devastating possibility.

After those initial inclinations, the question came again, but this time as if God himself was asking, "What do you *really* believe about me, Kevin?" It seemed a deliberate inquiry as if he were sitting next to me in the truck, leaning in to whisper directly into my right ear. I felt a million emotions coursing through my entire being, including anger, confusing my mind inexorably, making it ridiculously difficult to process such a profound, multi-faceted question.

It did not seem fair to ask such a question, much less require an answer right then in the face of such tragedy. Yet it had clearly been asked, causing a collision of circumstance with convictions I had previously believed were concrete. Yet nothing can feel concrete in such situations, right? Everything I thought was solid and secure inside was now shaking, as if internally I was experiencing a catastrophic earthquake. I knew for my own sake and my family's sake—it *required* a definitive answer if I were to face all that would crash upon us when we reached the hospital. Yet, it still did not feel real, so while I knew I would have to answer that question, I still wanted to believe it all was just a bad dream. So, I left my answer yet unclaimed and unspoken.

Glancing at my wife, who had her head in her lap as she still sobbed uncontrollably, I exclaimed that I loved her and would give anything to take away her pain. She could not respond; she could only rock back and forth in her seat, battling unstoppable sadness. I unsuccessfully fought back the tears as I grabbed her hand and, with a shaky voice, said to her, "We have to put our faith in Jesus because He is the *only* one who can bring our son back to us now." As I spoke the words, my soul shivered, vexed by whether I did believe that to be true or not.

I let go of her hand just long enough to hit the handsfree phone button on my steering wheel to make the first call to my lifelong friend Zach Bryant. I blurted out the bleak news we had received to that point, then asked him to pray for our son, whose middle name is Zachariah, a namesake in honor of Zach, who is one of the most important people in the world to me. I implored him to tell his parents to pray, to put Mark on the prayer list at his church, to tell all his friends to pray, then told him I would let him know when we knew anything more and hung up.

I called my parents next, giving the same short news and making the same request: to call everyone they know and get them to pray for our son. My wife and I knew the only real action we could take for our son at that moment was prayer directed to the heavens above on his behalf.

The drive from that church gym to Greenville Memorial Hospital was the longest 16 to 17 minutes of my entire life. I continued to spontaneously pray out loud—begging Jesus to be with Mark, to hear our cries for mercy, to honor our request for a miracle, to spare his young life.

I remember growing increasingly anxious the closer we got, as adrenaline was pumping like a bubbling acid throughout my entire body. What was waiting for me, for us, over the next few hours and days? I felt so weak and unprepared to face whatever may come next.

> **Every trial we meet throughout our lives expands our endurance and fosters our faith.**

I did not know what to expect nor what I would have to bear because I had never faced anything like this. Then again, there in the darkness of my truck, with the blue glow from my dashboard seemingly the only light in the entire world, I was reminded that we had faced a great deal of adversity throughout our lives. Yet, every trial we met before had expanded our endurance and fostered our faith.

Wildly extreme thoughts continued to pop profusely in my head as we neared our destination, as if two enormous titans engaged in a brutal tug of war. One pulled for hope and peace, shouting chants of comfort, while the other yanked for despair and war, screeching mantras of menace.

For certain, the previous ordeals and outcomes of my life seemed to pale in comparison and could not begin to take away the pain nor offer any understanding of what we were facing.

We pulled into the ER parking lot, jumped out, and practically ran through the doors. Once we passed through the metal detectors and security, an extremely annoying delay when we were so desperate to get to our son, we were quickly met by a nurse who escorted us to a private waiting room.

Shortly after that, Hannah arrived at the hospital and made her way to that same waiting room with us, and as soon as the nurse left the room, she broke down as well. Dismay and doubt dripped from the very walls within, like melting wax from a candle burned far too long.

A waiting room is one of the most difficult places to be for anyone facing anything critical in nature. The torture is in the name—"waiting" room. Waiting for about anything is hard; waiting to find out the fate of a loved one is the *worst* waiting in all of existence.

The nurse returned after a few minutes to share that Mark was receiving initial brain and chest scans and that they would have to address his head injuries in the Emergency Room. After that, he would be transported to the Critical Care Unit (CCU), where he would remain for the foreseeable future. She went on to say the doctor would be in as soon as possible with the latest news and the next steps to address his condition. She asked if she could bring us water, to which we said, "yes, please," and she left the room to retrieve it for us.

As soon as she closed the door, the tears flowed again from Crystal and Hannah as they held each other while I tried to direct all our thoughts toward hope and trust in Jesus. It was all I could do, but it was so hard to look into the eyes of these women who love my son so deeply and see such fear, such heartache, and feel so helpless to take it from them.

We waited for seven to ten minutes, though it felt like years, and a doctor finally arrived. He greeted us politely, asking who each of us was before he began his explanation. He confirmed that Mark had experienced multiple cardiac arrests and had been oxygen deprived for up to 15 minutes. The doctor then conveyed that Mark also sustained a head injury when he fell, initial scans had been performed (and they were waiting for results), and finally, he had not regained consciousness. We then left that waiting room as they guided us down a series of corridors into the Emergency wing, where they cared for Mark and would clean him up for whatever would come next.

As we approached his room, every step I took shot impulses of dread from the bottom of my feet to the tip of my skull. My entire heart felt coated in concrete—every heartbeat within me was the heaviest, most labored I had ever experienced.

The gravity of life can strike like a lightning bolt, violently splitting a tree to its roots.

I struggled to keep my breathing from racing out of control and hold down the distress that surged within me as I prepared to look upon my son. As I crossed through the door and reached his side, my eyes converged on his face—an image that scorched through my retinas and forever singed itself onto my soul.

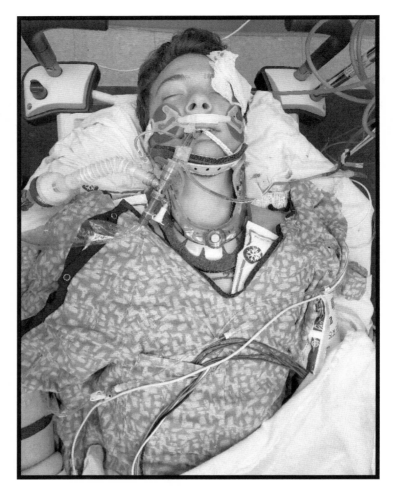

***First look at Mark Clayton in the Emergency Room
on Sunday, November 10th, 2019***

The gravity of Mark's condition struck me like a lightning bolt violently splitting a tree to its roots. I felt paralyzed and on fire at the same time.

Fateful Falling

Once again, because of my photographic memory, I immediately knew this was an image that would force itself upon me sporadically and without warning for the rest of my life. Imagine the worst post-war ruins you have ever seen; smoke, darkness, wreckage—death as far as the eye can see. Now imagine searching the rubble, only to come across the body of your lifeless child. This scene is what materialized within my mind as I gazed upon my son.

The left side of Mark's face was bandaged from head injuries he suffered when he passed out and fell to the ground. Blood still covered that side of his head, soaking the gauze and transferring to the sheets on the bed. A breathing tube protruded from his mouth, pumping his lungs up and down to keep my son alive, yet the mechanical nature and calculated rhythm felt so forced and lifeless at the same time.

Mark's neck and head were held firmly by a complete brace system. IV tubes intruded on his veins in both arms, dripping medicine and hydration fluids into his immobile body. Wires ran everywhere, connected to machine pads on his chest and head to monitor his vitals. Ice packs lined both sides of his lungs and chest to protect his body from the fever trying to flare within him.

Finally, I noticed that his wrists were firmly strapped to the side of the bed rails to inhibit him from involuntary movements that could further harm himself or others. That was the one factor that affected me more acutely than anything else I had just observed.

Death had stolen away my son for up to 15 mins as he laid lifeless on the ground—now he was being held prisoner by it still, strapped to its frightening threat of finishing what it started back at the gym.

Tears imposed themselves into my eyes as I inhaled slowly, resolutely mustering whatever I could from my fragile spirit. I reached up, put my hand on Mark's forehead, and leaned into his right ear, saying, "It's Dad, Mark; I am here, and I will not leave your side." It was clear that a fight for life was fully in front of us, and it would involve fear, fury, and faith like no fight I had been privy to ever before.

The room was buzzing like a beehive, a myriad of doctors and nurses performing various tasks on our son. They asked us many questions, trying to piece together all that happened so that they could provide the best care, yet we had not even had a chance to put together all the details ourselves in all the chaos. Sam and his friends were the only people who had any context around Mark's collapse, but we had not been able to speak to any of them up to that point.

In the medical fray, one of the head doctors in charge made his way past the other team members and over to Crystal, Hannah, and me. Politely while sympathetically introducing himself to us, he asked if anyone informed us of facts known so far, to which we answered that we understood all those details.

After a few moments of watching and listening to my son's heart and lungs with his stethoscope, he looked at me, then asked if he could speak to me separately. He pulled me aside to the dark corner of the room, just out of earshot of Crystal and Hannah.

I knew what was coming and what he was going to say before the words formed in his vocal cords and exited his mouth.

"Kevin," he said, pausing to prepare himself to speak what he must and placing as much care as he could on his face.

Fateful Falling

He gravely began saying, "This is going to be difficult to hear, but I see these women you care for here (pointing behind in the direction of Crystal and Hannah), so I need to prepare you. You need to understand that if your son was oxygen-deprived for up to 15 minutes, there is a strong chance that even if he does survive, he will probably have severe brain damage."

Continuing, he said, "Your son will not likely ever come back to the way he was before he collapsed if he survives at all."

He ended with, "I hope and pray he lives. I am so sorry for you and your whole family."

The instant he finished, I remember three feelings hit as if bullets had just peppered me from out of the gun which death coldly held pointed at my son, me, and my entire family.

The first feeling to pierce me was sympathy and gratitude for this doctor who had to convey such terrible news to a grieving father and family; he had done it with concern and grace yet held to the facts that had to be communicated. Evidently, this was not his first such news brief, and that experience enabled his calm, steady delivery. I applaud you, doctor, for I could never do what you do day in and day out—I am grateful for both your expertise and the sincere compassion you were able to craft in your words and body language tied to such a tough message.

The second feeling that ripped through me was the foreshadowing of a void that may forever establish its empty expanse in all our souls if my son's heart stopped beating for good, forcing us to live the remainder of our lives without him. The world at large would permanently darken a bit from such a loss, and our world would forever be changed with only a dim silhouette of where our son used to stand. I could not then, nor do I *ever* again, want to fathom such a world.

The third and final feeling bore hard quickly, but it was not like the others. I said aloud to the doctor, "Thank You, I appreciate your honesty and prayers." Yet the defiant response my soul fashioned within while remembering his words that my son may not survive at all was, "Maybe so, but I know someone who came back from the dead, and He is here with us right now!"

> **"Faith is deliberate confidence in the character of God whose ways you may not understand at the time."**
>
> **—Oswald Chambers**

I walked back across the emergency room to stand at the foot of Mark's bed and stared directly into the lifeless face of my son. Then it came again, the question that had been asked of me in my truck on the way to the hospital. But this time, it was even more personal and pointed. It felt as if Jesus Himself was standing behind me now, leaning slightly into the back left side of my body as He spoke in a strong yet subtle voice saying, "Who do you believe I *really* am, Kevin?"

There was no evading the question now. My humanness wanted to respond with, "Seriously? You would make me answer that question right now, while I am wrecked, with my son laying there dead and gone in front of me?" Yet as soon as that question came into my head, the next quickly followed: What do I believe?

I have claimed countless times throughout my adult life that I believe in Jesus. But the question this time did not merely ask, do I believe *in* Him, but rather, do I believe *Him* as a living, genuine savior? Not to believe in the mere *idea* of Him or the misconceptions of who others believe Him to be. To move beyond the notions of Him as the unusual priest from thousands of years ago who said and did all those bizarre things which are so hard to believe; or as the outdated, overrated, old-fashioned, obsolete leader which the world-at-large paints Him to be all too often.

No, His question was pointed to me, as a question of *identity*, as to *who* I believe Him to be. Everything I had ever believed was on the line, right here, right now, and I had to decide.

Early 20th-century Scottish teacher and chaplain Oswald Chambers once wrote, "Faith is deliberate confidence in the character of God whose ways you may not understand at the time."

I thought I knew the character of God; I had studied and sought it for years, but how could He now allow such heinous tragedy to enter my life?

While I did not have answers to what presented itself, which is truthfully the state we live in most the time, I knew it was time for a decision. I conclusively and purposefully planted a stake in my soul, saying in a low audible murmur, "I know who You are. You are the way, the truth, and the life (John 14:6). I believe You, Jesus, that *You* can save my son if You so choose. Yet if You do not, I will trust You must have Your reasons."

I *chose* to place my trust in Jesus, knowing He has armies of angels at his beck and call and strength enough for everyone now faced with the possibility of Mark's life slipping away.

At that moment, I understood what I had pushed to the side of my psyche at the bottom of the stairs before leaving our house earlier that night. I honestly believed in the deepest part of my being that Jesus was about to do something crazy amazing, a miracle, as I stubbornly refused the notion that God would grant death its demands for my son.

Perhaps such belief was merely the foolish whim of a father—but what if it was something else, a notion or nudge from the realm unseen? I was not sure which was true, but I decided to cling to this defiance, depending upon its potency, until arriving at the outcome of my son's fateful falling.

CHAPTER II
A FIGHT WITH DEATH

Faithless is he that says farewell when the road darkens.

— J.R.R. Tolkien, The Lord of The Rings

Death still sickly smiled behind its smoking gun, believing it had perhaps delivered its final kill shots after the doctor's ominous news to me there in the corner of the ER room. I returned to Crystal and Hannah's side to continue comforting them; however, something was different inside me. I was furious at death, and boldness now spread through my veins as I insolently streamed another silent prayer to Jesus in heaven above, "Jesus, bring Mark back to me, to us. I believe You have power even over death itself, so I humbly beg You, save him, and *BRING HIM BACK TO LIFE!*"

A bit more time passed, then a different doctor came in to put stitches in the large cut that Mark sustained over his left eye when he had fallen. As he removed the gauze from his head, the cut was gaping wide and while the gushing bleeding had stopped, I caught a clear glimpse of his skull itself right over his eye which was another stark reminder of how severe the situation was. The doctor executed the stitches perfectly, then shortly after came the news that they would be moving him to the CCU as they escorted us to another waiting room right next to the CCU wing of the hospital.

RISE! MIRACLE THROUGH A FATHER'S EYES

As we arrived in the new waiting room, I remember the overhead lights came on as they functioned on motion sensors, which felt like an abrupt interrogation. I did not want a shred of light to shine on me. I did not want anyone to see the grief that alighted on my face; instead, I wanted every bit of light in the world pointed at Mark to help him find his way out of the dark abyss that currently held him tightly in its cavernous grip.

We sat for a few minutes, just the three of us, then the elevator doors opened, and out came Mike, Andrea, and Sam, who had been waiting for news while down in the Emergency Room for quite some time. Those tearful embraces with first Mike and then Andrea were so important to me because they had been great friends since we arrived in South Carolina.

When I got to Sam, still visibly shaken by the whole ordeal, I held him tightly and thanked him with the deepest gratitude I could offer for springing into action—kneeling over his friend while performing chest compressions to try and keep him alive. I knew it would be hard, but I asked him to relay the story from his perspective as we needed as much information as possible to help the doctors with imminent decisions to try and save Mark's life.

Sam explained that Mark had told his friends he was running out to the car to get a Gatorade to address his low blood sugar level (Mark has Type 1 diabetes, aka T1D) and shot out the side door of the gym. After about eight to nine minutes of Mark not returning, one of his new basketball buddies he had just met that night, Zach Byer, went out to check on him and found Mark on the ground, unconscious and bleeding. He rolled him over and called 9-1-1, which likely took 1 to 2 minutes just as Sam drove up to the building. Seeing what was happening, Sam jumped out of the car, ran over, and immediately started chest compressions.

A Fight with Death

Sam continued filling in all the blanks for us, stating that he kept up chest compressions for what he said was about 3 to 4 minutes before the paramedics arrived. Combining that with the knowledge of what the EMT had told me at the church— basically that they had to work on him for a bit to get a heartbeat back in my son—the whole picture was getting clearer and direr at the same time.

> **The grim weight of the scale was tipped cripplingly to one side with statistics that did not favor survival.**

I quickly did the math of the minutes Sam conveyed, which confirmed a range of 13 to 15 mins that my son could have been unconscious without oxygen. As Sam finished talking, I believe everyone in the room now felt it—the grim weight of a scale tipped cripplingly to one side with statistics that did not favor Mark's survival.

A brief time later, my son Brian arrived in the waiting room accompanied by Justin Crucey, a friend to both my sons. Another round of embraces ensued, and the collective shock we all were experiencing was palpable in the air of that waiting room.

Not long after that, Connor Hash (who was one of the other young men at the gym earlier that night) and his then-fiancé now bride Courtney showed up to support us as well, even though Connor had just met Mark that night for the first time (which says something about your character Connor so thank you).

After talking for a little bit, I gathered everyone in a circle to pray. We prayed for wisdom for the doctors, nurses, and surgeons who would diagnose, care for, and perhaps operate on my son over the following hours, days, weeks, and maybe even months. We prayed for God to intervene—to save his life and bring healing. We prayed for strength because every one of us was incapacitated at the thought of Mark never opening his eyes again. None of us knew what the timeline or aftermath of his critical condition would be at that point, medical staff included.

> **He was now in a place where no one except God Almighty could reach him.**

We prayed for a few minutes before I cracked my eyes and noticed that one of the primary doctors had joined us, patiently waiting for us to conclude our prayers. I said, "Amen," and then we all huddled around the doctor to hear what news he was bringing.

He explained that Mark was running a high fever due to the cardiac arrests and trauma to the rest of his body and brain. After considering the fact that he had been oxygen deprived for so long, combined with the brain swelling resulting from the head injury when Mark fell, he announced his plan.

To minimize damage to Mark's brain and give him the best chance for survival, he believed they needed to place him in a medically induced coma for 72 hours and utilize a "chilling machine" to reduce and control his overall body temperature during those three days. He expounded on the necessity of this machine to keep the life-threatening fever at bay, reduce the brain swelling as much as possible, and maximize oxygen and healthy blood flow while he rested.

A Fight with Death

They would take his body temperature down and maintain it at a specific degree range for 24 hours; then, if he were still alive, they would slowly increase his body temperature over the next 48 hours until it reached normal 98.6 degrees. However, he also informed us that because Mark had not regained consciousness at any point so far, the coma meant that they would not be able to ascertain if he had any brain activity whatsoever until the 72-hour period had concluded.

Hannah conferred with Crystal and me, then together, we provided approval for the doctor to proceed. As the doctor walked away and passed back through the doors into the CCU, I knew that we were literally placing Mark into God's hands for the next 72 hours; three days, ironically enough. He was now in a place where no one except God Almighty could reach him. I took a deep breath and asked Jesus to protect and be with my son during every moment of his unconsciousness.

The clock was moving on, now about 10:45 p.m., and I dismissed myself from everyone in the waiting room to make a few more phone calls, as I knew others who had not yet heard the news would want to know.

I first called my brother, Chris Clayton, to relay all my information to this point. My brother understands better than most just how close I am to my boys. We spent many years together living in North Idaho from when my sons were born in 1998 and 2000, before we moved to Chicago for three years back in 2013, and then on to South Carolina in early 2016.

Chris and I had had many late-night conversations about fatherhood, we had watched them play in an insane number of basketball games over the years, and we had shared in legendary nerf gun wars in my house and yard. We had moved all the furniture against the walls in my living room to throw down mattresses and pillows to create our very own amphitheater for Roman gladiator-style wrestling matches.

In addition, we absolutely ruined many small nerf basketball hoops that I had mounted on a wall over the office door in our home for epic dunk contests that usually ended up with someone mildly getting hurt or a wall needing repairs of some kind. You see—these are the kinds of memories that pop into one's mind when your child's life is at risk.

When I finished telling Chris the medical status of Mark, we both wept as he kept saying that he could not believe this was happening. He loves his nephew and fully understands how much I love my son, so he knew what kind of pain I felt as I emotionally stumbled through the conversation. He consoled me while reminding me of all the hard things my family has faced over the years and expressed that we are "uniquely equipped" to deal with this, encouraging me that God was with us and was still all-powerful even in this.

He prayed for me over the phone and then said he wanted to come down to be with us during this time. I tried to tell him I understood that it was expensive coming across the country, as he would be coming from the Northwest where he lived, but he said, "Don't worry about that; God will provide, and I will make it happen. I will get you the details of when I will arrive as soon as I can arrange everything." As I hung up, I felt relief because inside, I knew that I needed support, and it would be good to have my brother here to face the looming uncertainty with me.

My next call was to another lifelong friend, Brian Parker, whom I had met in high school and had drawn close to throughout our college years and beyond. My youngest son is named Brian, again as a namesake to honor him as a friend who has profoundly impacted my heart and life since I was 16. He has been with us through many of life's ups and downs and offered true friendship. I gave him the news of Mark's condition, and he offered his sympathies and shock over the situation. He also reminded me of the many hardships we had endured over the years, specifically recalling that we had almost lost our son Brian when he was a young toddler—another profound story for a different time.

He also prayed for me over the phone and then surprised me by asking if he, too, could come down to South Carolina to be with us during this time. As he also lives in the Northwest, I again explained that I understood it was difficult and expensive to travel cross country on such short notice. Still, he did not care, stating he would get to us as quickly as possible and let me know when he would arrive. I remember feeling deeply grateful for the sacrifice that both he and my brother were willing to make; it truly meant a great deal to me.

My next phone call was to Ryan Hadden, another of my closest friends who lives in the Northwest. The weekend before my son's accident, I spent three days with him and four other friends of mine for a much-needed "guys getaway" at a vacation house on the ocean in coastal Lincoln City, OR. It had been set aside as a time for us to connect as friends, as brothers, to share where we were in our lives; to honestly reveal our feelings, our fears, our goals, our hopes, our dreams as husbands, fathers, friends, and imperfect followers of Jesus Christ.

We prayed, laughed, ate, spent hours upon hours talking, and walked the beach together, absorbing amazing sunrises and sunsets. It was a deep time full of meaning and camaraderie, after which I returned to South Carolina on Monday, November 4th, with a renewed strength and fervor for life. Then, BOOM! Just four days later, my grandmother, Willie Ann Schlaegel, passed away on Friday, November 8th, and two days after that, my son fell and was left fighting for his life.

Ryan was one of the few people who truly knew my state as a man at that point in my life, having just shared in that long weekend together, so as I relayed what was happening with Mark, he really could feel my angst and understand how deeply it hurt me as a father. He has a way of comforting others around him, which is core to how God made him, and I have always appreciated that in his character.

He listened and bore the depth of this tragedy with me, reminding me that God had filled me the weekend before as a precursor to pour out faith into what I was now facing. Ryan promised that God was present and would use it somehow, then he also prayed for me, which I welcomed because I needed all the prayer I could get. After he finished, he stated that he loved me and would be praying non-stop, then we ended the call.

After I hung up with Ryan, I took a few moments for myself in the darkness of the area by the CCU waiting room elevators. Thinking about all he had said to me, I felt something traveling up the roads from my heart to the highways in my mind in search of sanctuary. It became apparent in the next few minutes that God wanted me to tell this story as it unfolded—to share openly and viscerally what would transpire in the hours, days, or weeks to come with anyone and everyone who might be listening or watching.

> **Life's deepest convictions travel up from simple roads of the heart to busy highways of the mind in search of sanctuary.**

I knew this would not be easy because I wanted to hide this terrible pain, fear, and raw emotion spilling out all over everything and everyone. However, I also felt this inexplicable premonition that something was coming, an anecdote that would be riddled with amazement. I decided to use social media and email to impart the chapters of this tale as they happened in real-time, no matter how hard it may be, because there was too much at stake to be kept secret.

After making all the phone calls I could muster at the time, I left the waiting room and returned to Mark's room in the far back corner of the CCU wing, where my son's fate would be decided. I firmly believed that the key to his chances of survival would be the unbridled fervent prayer of as many people as possible. I sat in the chair next to my son's hospital bed, took deep breaths, and prepared to announce my son's state to a much larger audience.

I brought up the app on my smartphone, and there, in the center of the page, was the input field that flippantly states, "What's on your mind?" That question at that moment was like getting punched in the face. How do I conceivably answer that seemingly simple yet ridiculously complex question? I frowned and shook my head in response to this shameless inquisition and then dove headfirst into this "status" post.

I clicked in the field, and then with a thousand words racing around my head like a car burning laps at the Daytona 500, I started tapping letters on the screen keyboard. I struggled to type out the right words to let people know what had happened to my son while trying to see through the tears attempting to build a watery wall between my eyes and the screen.

At approximately 11:45 p.m., on Sunday, November 10th, I completed penning my first social media announcement. I hit "Post" to send this first message into cyberspace and out to the world of people connected to me.

It is with a heavy heart that I come asking for your prayers desperately. My oldest son Mark collapsed just a few hours ago playing hoops with his friends and was unresponsive for 15 mins. The paramedics were able to get his heartbeat back, but we are at the hospital now. He had two cardiac arrests, and he has been placed in a medically induced coma for the next three days while they keep his body temp chilled to limit the effects of oxygen deprivation in the rest of his body.

The bottom line is our son is literally in Jesus' hands for the next 3 days, as we won't know anything for sure until they bring him back out of the coma.

I love my son; so many people love my son... we are all in such sorrow right now but still trusting Jesus to walk our son out of this darkness of death and back into the light of life. Please join me in praying for my son Mark, his new wife Hannah, and our whole family right now.

Jesus, pour out Your grace, mercy, and healing to so many who need it right now, including my son.

Keep The Faith!!!

A Fight with Death

When I finished the post, I sent the same message via email to a support and prayer group I am part of, which consists of colleagues and friends I used to work with and other folks that members of the group are connected to via their business or personal worlds. I was amazed at how quickly the outpouring of prayer and well wishes began to flow.

Armies are awakened through a single voice of earnest prayer.

Family and friends piped in their thoughts of concern, sorrow, and grief, along with their insistent language of hope, love, and encouragement to keep fighting in faith. I remember sitting in that rudely uncomfortable hospital chair, feeling more compellingly comforted than perhaps at any other point in my life. Little did I know that I had just awakened an army, an army that now stretched far beyond just Greenville, SC.

I stayed with Mark in the room for an hour or so until Crystal called to let me know that several of our friends were leaving for the evening. There was not much more anyone could do this night, and it was apparent everyone was spent emotionally, with some having to return to work the next day. I went to the waiting room and saw that Nikk Butler had arrived with his then-girlfriend Samantha Yeargin. I hugged them both as they explained that they would be staying in the waiting room the rest of the night to support us.

Nikk and Mark had become close friends during their Senior year of high school and remained so after graduating, with Nikk always coming over to our house to hang out, eat, and play video games with our sons. He is like an adopted son to us, and I could tell he was devastated by what was happening to his friend. I hugged all our other friends who were leaving, thanked them profusely for their support, and said goodnight.

Hannah and Crystal settled in on couches in the waiting room to try and get some sleep, as neither would even begin to entertain the idea of leaving the hospital. After settling them, I returned to the CCU room to be with my son. As a lifelong night owl, God built me for "late night," and I already knew sleep was just not in the cards for the time being.

Mark is a social kid who hates to be alone. Anyone who knows me knows I have always had a special bond with Mark and an ability to get through to him in any situation, so there was no way I was leaving his side in this darkest time of his life.

I knew that there would be tough things ahead in that hospital room, and I wanted to shield everyone else from as much of that pain as I possibly could. Every father knows where I am coming from on this point—it was *my* responsibility to be there for my son, to bear those onerous burdens with and for him, while I protect my family no matter the cost to myself.

The nurses and doctors had explained earlier in the evening what to expect from someone in a medically induced coma. One of those expectations was that his body would react involuntarily at times. Since he had not regained consciousness after his fall and cardiac arrests, his body and mind were still likely pushing to "wake up," which would result in twitching, jerking, or possibly even full-blown seizures. That was frightening. I knew it would be impossible to predict those reactions, so I would have to be on constant watch, like an old castle guard on high alert, looking for any movement that could be a threat.

A Fight with Death

The first time he had a big involuntary reaction, it was one of the *hardest* things I have ever experienced as a man, much less as a father. His back arched, his chin turned toward the ceiling, and his shoulders pushed forward off the mattress. With his wrists still strapped to the bed, this motion contorted his body in a way that looked so painful and unnatural.

I leaped into action, immediately putting my left hand on his forehead, draping my body and right arm across his, and speaking loudly right into his ear, saying, "Everything is ok, Mark, it's Dad. I am right here, son. Just relax, I love you, you'll be alright."

I did not know if that last statement was going to turn out to be true or not. Still, I did know scientists have proven that people in comas can often hear what is said aloud, so I was going to speak hope, positivity, and support into his ears every chance I got.

I held tightly onto his forehead and kept repeating those exact phrases over and over until his body finally relaxed and returned flat on the bed. His reaction was probably only 15 or 17 seconds, but it felt like hours. I spent the next few minutes praying and reciting bible verses from memory into his ear. When it felt like he had calmed down completely, I stood up and spoke a bit with the nurse, who assured me that the reaction he had just undergone was normal. At least now I knew what to expect and felt a bit more prepared for the next one, which would inevitably come.

I remember feeling extraordinarily restless; I wanted to help Mark so desperately, yet I seemed helpless. It was a strange sensation not to be able to reach my son for the first time in my life. His body was right in front of me, yet his spirit seemed lost—a million miles away.

Each time I closed my eyes, it felt as if I was left pushing through the darkest forest, so thick with trees that it was difficult to walk at all, as I screamed my son's name, searching desperately for him. I so wanted him to suddenly open his eyes and exclaim that this was all just a joke. I would have gladly traded my life without delay to see my son restored to the living.

I watched Mark without a wink of sleep, barely allowing my eyes even to blink as his room was in constant motion. With Mark having Type 1 diabetes, that factor alone meant they had to check his blood sugar levels constantly, which resulted in the nurse coming to the room every 15 to 20 minutes for one thing or another. It was both reassuring and worrisome because each time, there came curiosity about what they were doing and what it meant. Fortunately, the nurse was excellent about communicating with every visit to help keep my worry as minimal as possible.

Mark had multiple similar involuntary episodes over the next few hours; consequently, my actions and phrases spoken into his ear were identical each time. I wanted him to hear my words repeatedly, to reassure him, to propel into him whatever peace possible as he journeyed through the jailing labyrinth of his coma.

After a few episodes and ensuing conversations with the night nurse, it became evident to them that I was willing to do anything for my son. That said, it led to their granting me a bit more freedom in the CCU room than perhaps they usually would allow a parent in helping to provide care. I will forever be grateful for that leniency because Mark needed me—truth be told, it was also because I needed to be *actively* involved rather than being rendered a spectator during this battle for his life. I am not a doctor but a warrior by nature, so I knew I could help my son by being present fully and unreservedly, as I had been his whole life.

> **Better to be a warrior than a spectator during any battle for life.**

Thank God this event took place before the nightmare of COVID-19 in 2020 because I probably would have landed in prison tied up in a white coat and cinched down to a bed of my own if they had told me I could not be with my son. My heart goes out to each person who has had to endure a hospital stay or brave the loss of a loved one without being able to be right by their side. I have prayed so many prayers for all of you—because I can understand and empathize with how hard that would be!

As the black of night turned to the first light of day on Monday, November 11th, I was relieved that Mark was still alive and had made it through the night without any clinical seizures. I knew it would be a full day ahead, hopefully providing much-needed answers, so I was excessively anxious.

What made my son's heart stop in the first place? We did not know if it was related to his T1D or if it was a heart condition, a freak accident, or some other medical mystery. Having been an athlete and in good health his entire life (except for the T1D), my mind kept repeating the inquiry of what made his heart stop like a broken record.

Hannah and Crystal were awake again and back in the room to be by Mark's side. Throughout the day, the medical team came to get him multiple times for various procedures, including both an EKG and a full chest X-Ray. The time between those procedures when we were in the waiting room was difficult to navigate emotionally. We all knew that his condition could change in the blink of an eye, so we did our best to comfort each other, praying without ceasing. Each passing minute was a hybrid, holding both the angst of waiting to understand what happened to our son and the relief of being able to continue clinging to hope for his survival.

By late afternoon, the medical team converged upon the CCU room, and we would receive definitive news on Mark's condition. Finally! We had concrete information, a culprit of the cardiac arrests—Wolff Parkinson White (WPW) Syndrome. When the cardiologists first disclosed this diagnosis to us, it sounded so bleak; the use of words like "rare" and "abnormal" shocked me like 220 volts of electricity shot straight into the soul.

Listening intently, we worked hard to push our feelings aside in favor of facts, a pursuit that I dare state is worthwhile in every circumstance that life thrusts upon us. As they talked through the details of what WPW does to the heart, we were able to mine out the gold nugget we were waiting for; it was a *curable* condition! Even though my son laid silent and insensible just a few feet from us in the room, it felt as if he were not so far away in that instance, thanks to this hope that surgery could cure the WPW ailing his heart. However, that sensation was quickly tempered with the fact which came next.

They went on to state that the chances of WPW being the only thing wrong with his heart and the singular cause of such catastrophic cardiac issues were improbable given his young age, athletic history, and overall good health. Once again, the medical team thoroughly explained the fine points to us, allowed us to ask questions, and left us with raw truth mixed with optimism. No one could ask for more, even if the optimism seemed to be a reach outside of reality.

A Fight with Death

This latest report would confine me to a clashing dichotomy on the inside. Half of me was optimistic that they could address the WPW, and the other half was realistic that there might yet be other conditions undiscovered in Mark's heart, not to mention the complete unknown of his brain function. I chose to tip the scales of my intellect toward optimism yet again, thankful that we had exposed a significant health disorder hiding in his heart, but with the silver lining of curability. We all would clutch to that single data point unrelentingly as we prepared to persevere into the next phase.

After the medical team left, I found a few moments of solace to pen my second status update at approximately 4:00 p.m.

Mark is still in the cycle of keeping his body chilled to give all his organs a better chance against oxygen deprivation. At midnight tonight, they will prep to start warming him up and slowly bring him out of sedation over the next 48 hours.

To clear up confusion, Mark had two cardiac arrests, not heart attacks. That is actually good news because heart attacks do more damage to the heart than cardiac arrest when it just stops.

They performed a chest X-Ray and EKG, and he has been diagnosed with Wolff Parkinson White Syndrome. In short, the human heart is supposed to have one main path running down the center, taking electric signals to the heart to make it pump. This syndrome basically means that Mark has another path that has formed on the left outside part of his heart. That confused his heart with mixed signals and caused cardiac arrest. The excellent news is that it can be treated with surgery. They will go up a vein in his leg and onto his heart to cauterize or destroy that other path so there cannot be mixed signals in the future. He has probably had it since he was born, but it does not reveal itself until teens or early 20's. Only 1% of people with the condition have it end up in something life-threatening, so once again, Mark had to be in the top 1%!!! Good Grief, son!! :) That surgery can't happen until after 72-hours, and he is showing normal cognitive function.

As we start the climb out of sedation and the chill, please be praying against seizures as those could be very damaging or life-threatening. And the biggest hurdle remains his neurological state, which we cannot analyze until he is lucid again and conscious at the end of the 72-hour cycle that started last night.

A Fight with Death

PRAY FOR MARK TO BE HEALED
& 100% RESTORED!!!

Mark is at Greenville Memorial Hospital (Downtown) and can be visited anytime except 6 AM to 9 AM and 6 PM to 9 PM as those are shift changes, and they don't allow visitors in the room. We, of course, have someone there all the time in the CCU Waiting Room on the 4th floor.

Thank you, everyone!!

Keep The Faith for my son!!

Sharing the news with family and friends of WPW being a curable condition was like a fresh wind into the sails of this ship which had been forced out to sea and stranded the night before. Over several hours I continued to get responses to both my first and second posts from people all over the United States, which became like blood transfusions for my own heart.

We often underestimate what a simple acknowledgment of someone's pain will mean to them. I was genuinely thankful to be receiving words of encouragement that ranged from just a few words to photos to long entries offering prayers and admonishments of faith. I cannot aptly express how much I appreciated this interaction and the selflessness that so many showed. It is impossible to talk with everyone during such a crisis, so in this instance, I was appreciative of our modern forms of communication, which gave me the platform to reach many people with news and allow them to reach back in support immediately. I was both blown away and humbled by the growing army of people praying for my son.

> **We often underestimate what a simple acknowledgment of someone's pain will mean to them.**

As the afternoon rolled over to early evening, I remember how hard it was to watch Hannah at her husband's side as she sat gazing at him with eyes that begged him to respond. She was frantic for a reaction to her voice, a touch, to receive any sign of life from this young man she had married just months ago.

The same was true for my wife, Crystal. Her tear-riddled eyes and caring face implored her son, whom she had nurtured from womb to manhood, to reply to her prompts for him to wake and crawl out of the coma and back into her arms.

It brought back moments for me from when he was a little boy when I would catch her at his crib side just staring at her child as he slept, no doubt thanking God for this beautiful creation which had already brought so much life to us all. I would often join her side to stare as well, praying for this young lad and reveling in our joy to be parents to such an amazing little man.

Now, we stood at a different bedside, beseeching the same God who heard our prayers all those years ago to provide a way for that joy to continue for just another second, minute, hour, and day. Time becomes the most precious commodity in all of existence in such moments, more valuable than all the gold or silver one could unearth.

A Fight with Death

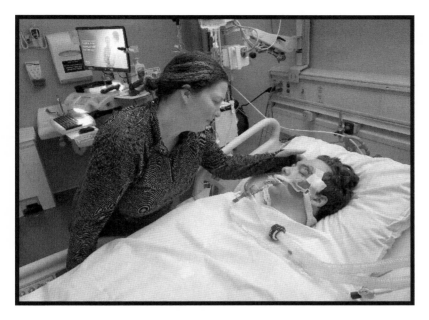

Crystal attending Mark in the CCU
on Monday, November 11th, 2019

As the late night approached, the ladies settled into chairs pushed together as make-shift beds in the waiting room for yet another night of broken sleep. Leaving the hospital was still not in the realm of consideration for anyone.

I hugged them both, kissed my wife and held her in my arms for a brief minute, and then walked back through the sliding door of the CCU. As I reached Mark's door, I paused and recall taking one of the deepest breaths I had ever inhaled in preparation for yet another sleepless night of watching over my son.

The second night would hold a new twist, as they would start the process of warming his body temperature back to normal over the next 48 hours. When they began the process, I held my breath as I put my right fist into my left, covering my mouth and then whispering a prayer into my hands, "Jesus, my son is lost somewhere in the darkness. As he begins this journey out of his coma, I beg you to take his hand and lead him home. Piece back together again what is broken in his brain, reach into his chest and hold his heart in your hand to keep it beating, speak to his soul that he may know You are there with him in the dark to show him the way out of this place he is in." I exhaled and took my place by Mark's side, beginning the process again of responding to his involuntary convulsions with prayer, comforting words, and scripture spoken into his ear.

Caring for my son was rough on my body as I had to lean over the hospital bed, contorting to hold him tight while being on my feet for prolonged periods. At the same time, exhaustion was starting to set in for me as I had not slept since the previous Saturday night, so it was getting more problematic as the minutes clicked away.

Mark has always had trouble sleeping at night (which he gets from me), so nights were always the hardest because his body seemed to fight more than at any point during the day—as if it knew he was missing out on life and hated the very idea of being unconscious. This sleepless game was nothing new for this boy of mine; even as a toddler, he did not sleep entirely through the night until he got into the first grade at about six years old. Yeah, that's right, six years old!

If you are a parent, you can fully empathize with a kid not sleeping through the night, but how many of you had to do it until they were six? My motto back then was "I'll sleep when I die," which I often said laughingly because of having to entertain this human pinball in the middle of the night. So, with that motto ringing in my ears once again, it was easy to adopt it now to be there with my son.

A Fight with Death

Mark and I had always been the nocturnal creatures in our family. We shared many great memories long after his mom and younger brother were sound asleep. In fact, Mark and I left the house entirely with those two sleeping more times than they knew to hit a late-night restaurant or movie over the years. Being with him at night had become customary for me, so even though these nights were hard in the hospital, I found it strangely comforting to be there with him during the period when most people were sleeping.

Hours went by, and my body was starting to cramp from the lack of rest and the circus act contortionist I was required to be over the last couple of days. I knew I had to sneak home for a few hours of sleep, and I also needed a shower. I have always been able to recover quickly, so just those few hours I knew would give me a respite. At around 4:30 AM on Tuesday, November 12th, I loaded up my backpack and then called Crystal to trade places with me in his room so I could make the quick trek home.

As I stood to leave the CCU room and glanced over at my son, I sensed the presence of death more potently than ever before in my life. I forcibly shook my head as if to say "No," then put on my coat and pulled my beanie hat over my head, which ironically had stitching with the letters P.O.D. on one side, which is the name of one of my favorite bands and stands for "Payable on Death." Wow—did those words take on a new meaning right then. I lifted my backpack from the ground, put my arms through both straps, kissed Crystal, and made for the door.

As I walked out of the CCU and stood waiting for the elevator, a thought flashed into my mind that I may have just left my son alive for the last time. Such are the uncontrollable thoughts that torture every human being in these circumstances.

They are impossible to stop; all one can do is not dwell on those terrible knives to the cortex but quickly dismiss them.

> **It is amazing how simple things can become difficult when one is in crisis.**

The elevator doors opened, then I walked in and turned around. As I watched the doors close, I paused for a moment, then hit the button to take me down to the main lobby.

It is amazing how small simple things like pushing an elevator button can become difficult when you are in crisis. As it headed down, the elevator felt directly tied to the gravity of my heart—by the time it reached the bottom, everything in me felt heavier. The doors opened, and I walked around the corner and down a hallway toward the glass exterior hospital doors.

When the weighty exterior doors opened, a wet, cold rush of air hit my face, as if the demon of death had just opened its foul mouth to breathe directly upon me, sending a frightful chill down my spine. I walked outside to an extraordinary blackness. After about seven or eight giant steps, I suddenly stopped and looked around slowly.

What I saw was a canvas that the grim reaper, with a sickle in hand dripping with ink dipped from a grave, had painted wickedly. From the gloomy ground below to the shadowy sky above, it felt as if this night had been ominously brushed just for me—to intimidate and horrify me.

I reached up at that moment, took hold of the cross that hung from the silver chain around my neck, and started walking quickly, as my breath created a fog moving away from my face with each exhale because of the cold. Never in my life had I encountered the presence of death so directly—it seemingly infiltrated my very veins.

As I reached my truck and opened the door to climb into the cab, I could no longer hold back the waters behind the dam of this tragedy, and the magnitude of it all broke, spilling over me. I fired up the engine, spun up the song "Flight" by Lifehouse on my stereo, then started my drive home, all the while trying to see the road through tears for my son, who just two days before had been so full of life but now laid comatose.

> **Music has the divine power to motivate the mind, move the body, and massage the soul in ways that all other forms of communication cannot.**

If you have never heard this song by Lifehouse I mentioned above, do yourself a favor and purchase it because it is powerful. The words in their song aligned perfectly with how I felt in that instance.

I always turn to music to be a loud voice to speak to my heart in life's most profound moments—it has the divine power to motivate the mind, move the body, and massage the soul in ways that all other forms of communication cannot.

As I drove, I could feel that I was beyond tired—I was utterly broken. My body throbbed in pain from head to toe, which I invited in a vain attempt to numb the pain I felt emotionally. I just wanted to get home, take two Aleve, and close my eyes for a short while. I felt so empty during that drive, as if everything that meant anything was absent. I knew it was not, but feelings are ferocious at times in their dominance of our psyche.

Upon reaching our house, I pulled into our garage, unsure of how I made it home awake, turned off my truck, and walked through the door into the living room, which was eerily quiet. I hated that! I remember saying aloud, "What I would not give to hear Mark's voice right now." I rounded the corner past our kitchen, down the hallway, and headed for my bed that awaited upstairs.

Brian (my youngest son) had been at our house with Kovu, Mark's black Golden Doodle puppy, who was not even a year old. He had gone to Mark's apartment after leaving the hospital on the first night to rescue and take care of him because Hannah had left in such a hurry for obvious reasons. When I got upstairs, I quietly opened the door to Brian's room and retrieved Kovu to take him into our main bedroom with me.

He was excited to see me, though he was sluggish from being asleep. I quickly went straight to the bathroom and fired up the shower water. Kovu followed, of course, sticking to me like glue. He could sense that something was wrong. Dogs have a sixth sense that way—no wonder they are called "Man's Best Friend."

I got the bed prepped and clean clothes ready while the shower was warming up, then went back into the bathroom, pulled back the curtain, and stepped in. I wondered for a second if Kovu would jump in the stand-up shower with me, but he was a good pup and laid on the floor right next to it until I finished.

The hot water on my body was such a welcome therapy. I have always loved water's power: to clean, quench thirst, and sustain life. I just wanted the water I was feeling right then to wash away all the pain. I stood there under the rushing stream, silent and still, for about eight or nine minutes. Thank God for the invention of on-demand water heaters, by the way!

I got out and tried to dry myself around a dog desperate for attention, then threw on clothes and fell into bed. No, seriously, I fell into bed. I could not hold myself up any longer—it was fatigue like none other I had ever felt.

Kovu quickly jumped up on the bed with me and stuck his face next to mine as I checked my phone for any messages. He has such sweet innocent eyes—it warmed my soul, and I had to snap a quick picture of his face. Kovu looked at me as if to ask, "Where is my daddy?" and "What is happening?" which was ridiculously hard.

Mark's dog "Kovu" lying in bed with me on
Tuesday morning, November 12th, 2019

As I petted and talked to this pup on my bed, I was thankful for him. Because you see, he was Mark's dog, and Mark loves that dog. It made me feel closer to my son. I also knew Mark would take immense pleasure in knowing that I was letting Kovu sleep with me on the bed because I had said when he got him as a puppy that I would never let that happen.

I could almost hear Mark laughing at me and accusing me of "being whipped by this pup" right then. I smiled and said to Kovu, "Your dad is fighting for his life. We are not giving up on him ever, ok?" He licked my face and then settled in next to me to get some sleep. I put my phone on the nightstand, took those two Aleve, and I promise I was out the second I shut my eyes. I got about three and a half hours of sleep in all.

When I woke, I felt surprisingly strengthened. I called Crystal to check on Mark and got the good news that he was still alive and progressing well in the process of raising his body temperature. I hung up the phone, took the dog outside in the backyard for a bit to get some of his energy out and love on him, then gave him back to Brian and headed to the hospital. During that drive back, I prayed that this fight with death would become an awakening.

CHAPTER III
AWAKENING

*Faith is taking the first step even when
you don't see the whole staircase.*

—Martin Luther King, Jr.

I arrived back at the hospital a little after 9:00 a.m., and there was again a sense of mixed emotions amongst us all. Mark was still with us, but we knew the real storm was coming, like a hurricane lurking just off the coast with its sight firmly set on making landfall. Every hour his body temperature rose without significant setbacks, we grew closer to understanding how bad his brain damage was and what else may be wrong with his heart.

As I looked at my son for the first time that morning, I noticed immediately that the medical team had rebandaged the side of his head while I was at home. His head looked much cleaner than it had to this point, which I was grateful for because it lent itself to the appearance of healing. I knew there was not any truth to that just yet, but it was still so difficult to see and touch him without getting back any sign of life. Each look upon his face incited a plea, "wake up and look at me, son!" from the deepest part of my soul. I was reaching for every splinter of hope that passed my eyes and every sound of possibility that floated into my ears.

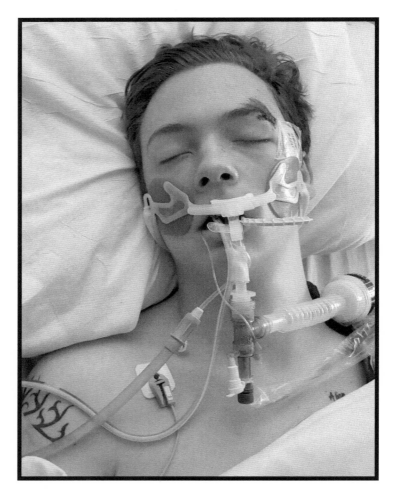

Mark in a coma in the CCU
on Tuesday morning, November 12th, 2019

I took a deep breath after staring at him for a few minutes and again put my hand on his head while praying into his ear, this time specifically for that day to come, begging that he fight hard and do his part to make his way back to life. I know my son, and I believed then (and still do now) that he could hear my heartfelt imploring for him to fight. I taunted him with whispers of challenge, informing him that some people thought his injuries and heart condition were too much to overcome and gave him little chance at best to survive.

Mark has always responded intensely to such challenges from critics who stated he could not do something. So now I was playing every angle I could think of to provoke him with psychological ploys to elicit a response in this—the roughest fight of his life. I quipped provocations directly into his eardrum, stating, "Are you going to let these people end up being right about you?" and "Don't you want to wake up and silence these doubters who say you can't come back from this?" mustering as much contest as I could in my voice. I wanted him to react in spirit the way he always had, by shaking his head while muttering, "oh-ho-ho-huh," almost laughingly, with a wildfire in his eyes as full acceptance of this challenge as an insult to his capabilities.

The process of taking his body temperature back up went faster than anyone anticipated, as we thought it would take more like 16 to 20 hours rather than just under 9 hours. As we approached 10:00 a.m., I penned out my third status update.

They have taken Mark's body temp back to normal over the last 8+ hours and are now beginning the slow process of adding nutrition to his system and slowly removing the sedation over the next 2 - 3 hours to get our first glimpse of his true condition.

Today is going to be a HUGE day, and we need everyone to pray specifically for a couple of things...

1) Please pray against seizures as he begins the climb back out of sedation; those could be seriously damaging or life-threatening.

2) Please pray that Jesus protected 100% of his cognitive functions and that every single brain cell be completely healed.

We feel the prayers of literally thousands of our brothers and sisters in Christ all across this nation and even on other continents! This is God's army...

When we stay focused on surrendering to Him, doing what is right, and living our lives with love first in both words and action, there is nothing impossible when God is with us and for us!

PLEASE PRAY HARD for these next hours that God will be mighty on Mark's behalf!!! Pray that Jesus will walk our son from the valley of the shadow of death back into the light of this life!

Awakening

We love you all and can't even begin to express what all your words of encouragement, the outpouring of love, and inspiring support have meant to us!

KEEP THE FAITH!!!

The medical team's first major effort of the day would be to start removing the sedatives from Mark's bloodstream to see what kind of response would result. The threat of seizures still skulked behind the bushes next to my son's bed, like a predator waiting for a chance to pounce. But we knew our son was strong and our God even stronger, so we all waited with bated breath as they began to bring him out of the jungle of this medically induced coma he had been wandering within.

Earlier the medical team had explained that his reactions could be erratic and even violent depending on his state, so we prayed hard and stared at him, trying not to even blink in search of any sign of consciousness. Minutes passed slowly, torturing us as if we were being forced to watch every grain of sand fall through the hourglass one at a time.

After a couple of hours of waiting, we grew ever more anxious. Then it happened. Mark arched his back and cracked his eyelids open, rolling his eyes forward from the back of his skull and moving his head from side to side rapidly, searching for something or someone recognizable.

Eruptions shot through every nerve of my body, and excitement boiled over within me. Miracle number one—my son had opened his eyes and found my own. I wondered if I would ever see that again, so I was ecstatic. Crystal and Hannah felt the same, as evidenced by their emotional responses.

I spoke loudly to him, "Hi Mark, relax, son, you are in the hospital, and we are all right here by your side!" with the most powerful voice I could rally.

For the next hour, I traded similar lines alongside the doctors and nurses working with Mark to respond. It was apparent the drugs still held his consciousness captive as he repeatedly tried to lift his arms awkwardly from the straps that held him down. Inside his glazed-over eyes was confusion, and he could not focus on anyone or anything.

He was clearly responding to commands by moving his head side to side depending on who was speaking, which was promising, but he continued to fade in and out of consciousness very abruptly. The doctor and nurse continued attempting to wake him. His stirring included the involuntary movement of his legs and feet, which was another positive indication that his mind and nervous system were still intact to some degree. However, he could not squeeze a finger or give a thumbs up on command.

I could tell that lack of response concerned the medical team, but they expressed positivity to all of us and kept us focused on the facts of the ways he *was* responding. After working on him for a few hours and successfully keeping any major seizures at bay, they determined the following medical procedure. They then left the room to put a short-term EEG test into motion. I snuck into the back corner of the CCU room and, at 3:00 p.m., quickly typed out my fourth update to the world of wonderful prayer warriors waiting for status.

Awakening

Mark has been opening his eyes and moving his legs somewhat over the last 2 hours. He also moves his head from side to side depending on who is talking. He still can't focus well, as he is still coming out of the sedation.

The neurology team just did their first exam, but because he is still under the sedation influence so they could not get conclusive results just yet. He did move his head on command from side to side and opened his eyes on command, but still could not squeeze their hands or give them a physical thumbs up. They ordered the EEG, which will be the first step in examining his brainwaves, and are prepping him for that now. The next step will be an MRI later (time TBD) to analyze his brain for the effects of oxygen deprivation.

We are encouraged, and just to see his eyes open gives us hope, but he still has a long way to go!! PLEASE PRAY HARD, family!!!

Stay tuned... KEEP THE FAITH!!

About 30 minutes after my update, they wheeled the machine into his room for the short-term EEG test and began to prep Mark. The neurology tech was a beautiful black woman who very caringly shared with us what she would do during this initial test of his brainwaves.

We asked a few questions to clarify what this test would reveal, then stepped back to allow her to examine our son. She quickly and concisely began to connect a network of multi-colored wires all over Mark's skull, which led up to the main panel above and to the left of his head. Once she had finished routing the web of wires, she wrapped his head in gauze to hold everything in place and began the test procedure.

I remember thinking that he would probably laugh at how he looked—making a comical comment about him becoming a modern-day Frankenstein. That brought a smile to my face amid watching this process unfold.

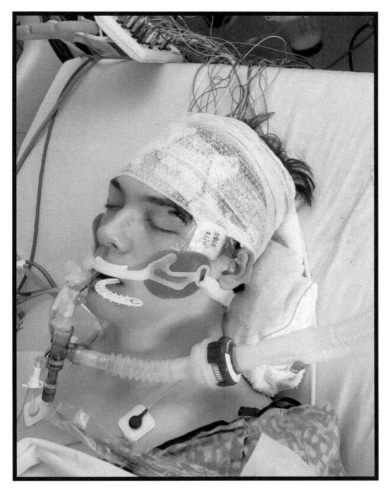

Mark undergoing a short-term EEG Test
on Tuesday afternoon, November 12th, 2019

I did not take my eyes off the tech the entire time she conducted her exam. She efficiently marched through her tests, going back and forth from looking at the results showing up on the monitor to taking notes on her computer. I was studying her body language, every muscle on her face, for a flinch or gaze that would reveal a positive or negative sign of my son's condition.

After moving through the various phases for about 15 minutes, I finally caught a reaction on her face. She raised her eyebrows while the slightest twitch of a smile snuck onto the corners of her mouth as she glanced over at Mark and then looked back at her screen. She caught herself, then quickly returned to a professional stoic state while completing her tests.

What she said next would be the second miracle we would receive this day. She carefully selected her words and then started to speak, saying, "It is too early to arrive at any conclusive results, so we'll have to wait for the full brain MRI regarding his overall brain activity. However, I must say that I am pleasantly surprised and amazed by the results I see here from this initial brainwave scan given the circumstances of his accident."

No words have ever been more welcome to my weary ears! I wanted to launch clear over the bed and throw a huge bear hug on her, but I decided not to scare her, instead letting my smile and body language provide my thanks.

She explained that a neurologist would look over the test results in detail and then get back to us later that evening to communicate the findings. She removed the wrap on Mark's head along with all the diodes, then said to him, "Good job, Mark, you hang in there and keep fighting, ok?!"

I was so thankful for a brief reprieve from the suffering. We were miles away from exiting this dark forest of death, but her facial expression during the test had forced a glint of light through the ceiling of those black trees holding their boding oppression over us. I broke into silent prayer once again, thanking God for this reminder that no matter how dark it was, there was a light strong enough to overpower it.

I leaned over my son and kissed his forehead, spurring him on by saying, "I see you, son, I know you are fighting. Do *NOT* stop! Come out of this darkness and back to the light. We are all waiting for you!" Feeling the good news, I sat in the chair next to his bed for a few minutes to collect myself and prepare for the next phase of this long road to awakening.

> **No matter how dark it is, there is a light strong enough to overpower it.**

The nurse returned to the room to explain that they wanted to continue trying to reduce the sedation to see how Mark would react in the coming hours. He was also still on heavy pain meds, which further complicated the accurate analysis of brain activity. However, they proceeded and began to measure his progress, warning us again that seizures were still a significant threat and could set him back immeasurably if he suffered one. I rose from my chair and took my place at his side.

Over the next couple of hours, he occasionally moved in and out of consciousness. Each time he did, the nurse or doctor present would ask him questions and ask him to do things. At around 6:00 p.m., we received a third miracle for the day when Mark made eye contact with a nurse and squeezed their hand on command—then he followed suit with me, Crystal, and Hannah over the next hour. This young man was fighting!

To feel a physical response to my request for him to squeeze my hand was nothing less than incredible. He did not know who anyone was at that moment. Still, he was showing signs of life, and more importantly, he was establishing a connection from hearing to *doing*, which was monumental on the long road to any form of recovery.

I hugged my wife so tightly, whispering into her ear, "Our son is a fighter; he is trying so hard to come back to us. We have to keep the faith that he will make it all the way back, honey."

A short while later, the neurologist returned to give us the details of the short-term EEG. He stated, ever so matter of factly, that Mark had passed the test "with flying colors," then said, "I am shocked given the circumstances of his accident and the oxygen deprivation that this initial test went so well. We still have to perform the full head/ brain MRI to determine what damage he has sustained conclusively. Still, I am extremely optimistic given these test results and his current state of responding to commands."

He explained that such favorable results on the EEG drastically minimized the chance of clinical seizures. In addition, he issued a responsible disclaimer that there is always the outside chance he could still have one but stated it was much less likely at this point. This news on the EEG would be the fourth miracle received in only a matter of hours from when they started bringing him out of the coma!

I could barely process my feelings at that moment, yet I knew God himself was with us, that He was there in that very room. All that had just taken place flooded my heart with new hope. I sat down in the chair next to his bed at 7:30 p.m. to type out my fifth update and share it with the growing crowd of folks following the story.

Awakening

Just 90 mins ago, Mark opened his eyes, looked at me, and squeezed my hand! He did the same for Crystal and Hannah as well. They did a short-term EEG to test his brainwaves, and he passed, so they did not need to do the long-term test! HUGE hurdles passed, and we are stoked!!

The next step is the brain MRI, and we are still waiting on a time for that, maybe tonight or tomorrow morning. He also has had no seizures, and they do not expect him to after passing the EEG that looks for seizure impulses... YES!!

This young man is a lion fighting hard, and Jesus is there with him fighting to get him all the way back to us!!

Keep praying, family; your prayers are being heard and answered!!!

KEEP THE FAITH!!

Upon successfully posting the latest status on the internet, I stopped to re-read it again. I wanted to see it with my own eyes because when I had left for a few hours in the early morning before dawn that same day—death had seemed almost invincible. Now I could claim that my son had looked at me with open eyes and squeezed my hand when I asked him! Just stop with me and re-read the post above one more time.

It is hard to completely understand a thing when you take it in second hand. But I cannot allow this moment to pass without giving credence to the incredible weight of the smallest things in this life and what they mean. I would have given anything in all the world to look into my son's eyes just one more time—to see and feel him respond to me.

> **Give credence to the incredible weight of the smallest things in this life and what they mean!**

Simple, trivial things are often what we take for granted with our family and friends every day when we are not in crisis. Please. *PLEASE!* Do not trivialize a simple gaze or a life-filled touch from whom you are blessed to have a relationship with. Those very things could be gone in the blink of an eye.

In keeping with this important truth, I want to draw attention to that second to the last line of my social media post from the previous page, precisely the phrase, "This young man is a lion fighting hard." I want to explain what this phrase means to me and allow you the insight of a deeper look into my past relationship with my son. Not to mention, a chapter devoted to such at this point will provide a bit of a reprieve from this heavy hospital saga at hand.

CHAPTER IV
THE LION'S ROAR

...a lion, mighty among beasts, who retreats before nothing...

—Proverbs 30:30

A lion's roar evokes immediate attention and commands absolute respect. Mark has always had an affinity for lions. It started when he was just over a year and a half old with the first stuffed animal (lion) I bought for him from FAO Schwartz in Seattle, WA while I was visiting there on a business trip.

I could never forget the way his big blue eyes lit up to marvel at this furry new friend I had brought home to him. As soon as he saw him, he reached out, threw his arms around its neck, and held him tight while making a few roaring sounds simultaneously—one of my many precious moments as this kid's father over the years.

He would carry that lion around for years to come, everywhere we went really, he had to have that lion by his side—whether it was going to bed, bath time, or traveling to faraway vacation destinations—he and that lion were inseparable. He ran around holding his lion by the tail, talking to him, and eventually used him as an entertainment prop when his younger brother would show up just a short time later in life.

However, the lion craze firmly took hold after he first watched the movie *The Lion King* by Disney.

I have never seen a kid as enthralled with a movie as Mark was with *The Lion King*. It was one of the only movies that kept his attention from start to finish *every* time. Now mind you, he could never sit still and *just* watch a movie. No. He spent half the time going back and forth from sitting on the couch to standing in front of the TV, dancing, singing, or acting out scenes as they happened on the floor of our living room. These antics of his are what I looked forward to—the show *he* put on every time made me laugh and entertained me thoroughly.

Once the movie was over, it became our time to play. "Mufasa, Mufasa, MUFASA!" I used to yell this phrase from the film, which the crazy hyena Banzai had coined to scare his other hyena buddies, and then I would chase Mark around the house acting like Mufasa while calling him Simba. He loved to reenact scenes from the movie with me, particularly the part where Simba would jump all over his dad on the ground because with Mark, the louder and more aggressive play time was, the better.

I would prowl into his bedroom, on all fours like a lion and roaring as I went, while he would sneak up on the couch in the living room behind me and then wait. I circled in and out of the bedroom, calling out, "Simba, where are you?" in my gruff lion voice. Then, as I rounded the corner in front of the couch, Mark would pounce on my back.

With his arms around my neck, I would buck wildly, trying to get him off as he laughed hysterically. Eventually, I would roll him off and tickle that kid mercilessly as I growled and bit at his belly. He never could get enough of that rough housing, and I cannot even begin to recount the hours we spent playing like this together when he was a toddler.

Candidly, I never could get enough of our playtime either—it brought me so much pure happiness. Listening to your child laugh, like a big belly roll laugh, is one of the most excellent sounds in all the world. It made life with all its adult struggles easier somehow.

Mark as a toddler, proudly wearing his
Lion King shirt in late 1999

These regular trips into innocence and connection taught me incredible lessons on child-like faith, acceptance, and love. I loved being a father back then, but only now am I understanding its fullness and what it has added to my soul since my sons were born.

> **The twinkle in your child's eyes,
> which appears as happiness and love
> pour out of them, is the purity and
> innocence we adults desire.**

I watched The Lion King hundreds of times with him during his childhood, so much so that I started to be haunted by it. I would get jarred from my sleep by Pumba (the stuffed animal who passed gas and then talked about it whenever anything moved his tail). I developed a facial twitch when I heard the phrase "Hakuna Matata" when out in public. Finally, there was a point where if I had stepped on one more Lion King plastic toy, I might have lost my mind and become a raging lion myself.

Those memories tied to annoyances still make me smile, though, because they remind me of the myriad of things we parents are willing to do and the lengths to which we will go to make our kids happy, even if it drives us crazy at times. Why? Because the twinkle in your child's eyes, which appears as happiness & love pour out of them, is the purity and innocence we adults desire if we are honest.

Back to *The Lion King*. The rote viewing of this single movie is where the lion itself took hold of my son. I could never have known back then the significance that the lion would hold for both of us in the future.

As he grew older, I began to speak more intentionally about the importance of the lion as King—a symbol of leadership, courage, loyalty, and strength. We would often talk metaphorically about his favorite movie, as I purposefully created parallels to his own life, which he could understand.

The Lion's Roar

I spoke of dangers that may threaten his life in the future. I referenced the elephant graveyard where death lurked and the importance of a lion pride protecting and fighting for each other. Lastly, I reiterated the consequences of not taking responsibility for who you are, as Simba attempted to do by avoiding his return home and failing to take his place as the rightful heir to the throne.

He *always* listened when I talked lions, which is probably the only thing I would say consistently grabbed his full attention. Other than the food—he was always aware of food just like his favorite animal would be—and he ate like a lion his entire life too. You should see this kid put away steak! Long live the carnivore (I am laughing right now as I write this).

His interest in lions continued to expand as he exited the toddler years, and now, he was interested in the actual animal. We watched Discovery Channel shows together, and he never failed to amaze me with his connection to lions. He was mesmerized by their magnificence, charmed by the playfulness of cubs, and hypnotized by their power as they hunted to bring down other huge animals. Enamored with this king of cats, he began to inquire about seeing the real thing up close.

When Mark gets something in his head, he can be relentless until he sees it come to fruition. It can be both exasperating and inspiring. He got himself in trouble countless times growing up because he wanted something badly and would not let it go when we told him no. On the other hand, he got to be a part of incredible things over the years because of his drive to pursue experiences in life.

One of my favorite experiences together happened back in 2007, when Mark was eight, almost nine years old. It happened at Cat Tales Wildlife Center; a small zoo focused on big cats north of Spokane, WA. Remember the lion which roared at the beginning of movies created by MGM all those years? If not, pick up your smartphone and Google it or YouTube it to check it out yourself. That astounding brute lived there at Cat Tales back then, and we would soon get to see him in person.

The day had arrived, and no shocker, Mark was ecstatic. The kid woke up early and bounced off the walls the entire morning. He would not shut up about seeing the lion that day. It was hilarious. At one point, I told him I would feed *him* to the lion if he did not pipe down and eat his breakfast! With breakfast successfully conquered, we made our way about an hour northwest of our house to Cat Tales, where upon arrival, Mark practically jumped out of our car before it even stopped.

We had to make a beeline for the lion first, as he was not interested in seeing any other cats until he saw *his* lion. That's right; it was *his*, not anybody else's! As we made our way toward the lion exhibit, I watched my son, taking in his excitement, wishing I could bottle up his energy for myself. Forget Red Bull; if I could have bottled up a drink called "Wild Mark," I would have made a killing in the energy drink market! Although I might have had trouble with continued sales— because people would never come down off the high of just one can of that crazy stuff.

When we finally arrived at the lion habitat, he rushed up as close to the cage as he could, yelling, "There he is, Dad," as he pointed emphatically at the huge mane-covered face staring back at us. My son stood there for 15 minutes just gawking intently at this furry friend of his—just waiting for something amazing to happen that he could turn into a story he would tell over and over. He did not want to miss a second of watching this awesome animal. What Mark did not know, however, was that we had an epic surprise in store for him.

The Lion's Roar

My Mom had researched and found that we could pay extra to feed the lion. When I heard this fact, I jumped at the chance to surprise my son and her grandson with this opportunity. You should have seen Mark when we told him he would get to feed the lion. His mouth dropped open as he started jumping up and down. It would be an understatement to say he was *beyond* excited.

One of the zookeepers pulled us aside and walked us through the process of what would happen with the feeding. The gentleman told us he would hand Mark a special pointed rod, the end on which he would put a raw cut of steak. Once the meat was firmly on the end of the rod, Mark would have to put it through a plexiglass hole in the chain-link fence to reach the lion's mouth.

He further explained that after the lion took the meat, he would need to pull the rod out for the zookeeper to put more meat on. They would repeat that process a few times to complete the feeding. He asked Mark if he understood, to which my son, with a big smile stretched over his face, yelled, "Yes," while trying to suppress his exhilaration and holding out his hand for the meat rod.

The last part of the instructions caught my son off guard. The zookeeper explained that Mark needed to be calm, not make sudden movements while feeding the lion and that he might feel a little scared while standing just inches away from the lion's huge head.

After hearing that, my son turned his head up and back at me (as I was standing right behind him) with a look that inquired, "Am I going to be able to do this?"

I said, "You can do this, buddy. I'll be right there with you." After getting that assurance, Mark looked back toward the zookeeper and said confidently, "I understand. I'm ready."

With the rod firmly in hand and loaded with meat, we started to walk up the concrete path toward the feeding area. Mark was in front of me, with the zookeeper to the left. As we got closer, the lion moved right up against the cage with its wide-eyed gaze fixed on my son—he could see the raw meat on the end of the stick coming his way.

With each step, the lion's head got bigger and bigger. When we reached the plexiglass, I remember looking directly into its eyes and feeling a chill roll up my spine. His head *was* huge! Now I was hearing, "Mufasa, Mufasa, MUFASA!" in my own head. It is one thing to look at them from a distance, but now just six inches away from this apex predator, I admit I was intimidated. If he had roared right then, I might have soiled my shorts.

Adrenaline was pumping through my veins as I became instantly aware of two things—first, I felt incredibly low on the food chain—second, my firstborn son was right in front of me, getting ready to feed hors d'oeuvres to this beast!

I said aloud to Mark, "Wow, he is a *big* dude!" He answered in a timid voice, "Yeah," as he stared upward into the face of his favorite animal. My son, very tall for his age, had to look up at this gigantic cat. I knew for sure he was feeling the same awe that I was.

With me beside him and the family behind him spurring him on, the zookeeper said it was alright to slowly lift the meat rod and put it through the plexiglass hole. When Mark reached out his arm, he was fully trembling. I assured him he was alright as I firmly kept my hands on his shoulders to help give him confidence and said, "Now you get to feed Mufasa!" A smile broke out on his face as he cautiously poked the rod through the hole and past the fence toward those jaws now dripping with drool on the other side.

Mark feeding a lion at Cat Tales Wildlife Center during the summer of 2007

Seeing the raw meat heading towards him, the lion dropped and angled his head to the side, then scrunched up its snout to reveal his teeth to grab his meal. I felt another chill go charging up my spine right as my son uttered a long, "*Woah.*"

I responded, "Man, look at those teeth, buddy!" He and I were both humbled as well as inspired to be so close to this King of the Jungle.

Mark pulled the rod back through the plexiglass hole to get a refill on the meat, then pushed it back through to the lion more confidently the second time. After that, his trembling went away a little more each time he did it, while his face grew more reverent. Watching the fear subside and the awe swell within my son as this incredible creature fed was the *best* part of the whole experience for me.

When the meat was gone, we took one last long look at the lion standing just inches away from us and then slowly backed away while we continued to face him as the zookeeper had instructed. Do you know what they say about not turning your back on the ocean? Yeah, an even more important thing to know is not to turn your back whilst the hungry eyes of a lion still stare at you—unsure if he perhaps sees *you* as the main course following hors d'oeuvres!

My son had a smile a mile wide. He gave me a huge hug, thanked me, then we slapped each other a high five as I said again, "You just fed the Lion King, buddy!" His face could not contain his elation as he returned to the rest of the family. They all made him feel like a hero as they hugged him, congratulated him, and asked what it was like to be so close to a lion.

I would wager only a few moments in this life have ever struck such a chord in my son as the experience of feeding a lion did. He talked about it for literally years after that. Now and then, we would get out the pictures from that day so he could reminisce about what it was like to stand in front of such a magnificent monster. He would remind me of how he felt scared at first but overcame that fear to stand face to face with his favorite of the entire animal kingdom—the lion.

In the years following, there were other lions as we visited zoos all over the country, where he would camp out for hours to watch them, as well as making me take photos and videos to commemorate his having been in their presence.

One lion, in particular, garnered his respect—Aslan, the king in the novel *The Lion, The Witch, and The Wardrobe* by legendary author C.S. Lewis. He loved the modern movie, which incited a deep talk about Aslan when he offers himself on the stone table to die, only to come back from the dead later in the story to defeat the white witch and her evil army. I had no idea how much this story would take root in the real world for him and me as we lived our lives.

Know your pride.

As the young years faded and Mark became an adult in his late teens, he and I shared new conversations about lions. As he grew, I used to say to him, "Know your pride." Your lion pride, as it were. This phrase was a provocation to genuinely *know* and *trust* the people who have earned the right to be in your inner circle; to honor family as well as those few true friends with how you live your life, how you care about their lives, and how you remain loyal no matter what. Regardless of who else is asking for a seat at the table in your inner circle before they have earned it, irrespective of what lies, slander, or gossip is voiced ignorantly or selfishly about you or someone you love—*know your pride*! In the end, those lion-hearted people, your pride, not the hyenas, will remain by your side no matter what life brings.

I would tell him, "You see, son, there are always hyenas; you know, the ones who claim to be your friend then laugh at your decisions, mock your integrity, feast on your failures, and attack you with arrogance but then somehow still feel you should include them in your pride. Really? NO," I would say, shaking my head, "*KNOW* your pride."

People who love authentically, do so without voiding truth, without being two-faced, without constant criticism, without envious exploitation, and without self-serving agendas.

Yes, we all make mistakes sometimes, but lion-hearted people strive to be selfless and serve, whereas hyena-hearted people steal out of selfishness and only want to *be* served. Big, *BIG* difference.

Mark and I had spent so many years talking about lions that now, with him being older, we wanted a more permanent way to share our connection to lions. So, we sat down one day and started talking about tattoos. All right, maybe you are not into tattoos. To each their own, I would ask that you please indulge me for a little as I share this part of *our* story with you.

I had only one tattoo to that point, a colorful tribal cross on my right arm, and Mark was looking to get his first one now that he was eighteen as a "grown-up" and "free man," in his own words. With that point cleared up (big wink), we sat down to design one tattoo that we could both ink onto our bodies, which would be slightly different for each of us.

We fashioned a design which was a set of four scratch marks—as if we had been clawed by a lion—with one of the scratches fashioned into a cross. Then we each selected a bible verse referencing a lion that we would place off to the left of the artwork itself.

The verse I chose was the last line of Proverbs Chapter 28, Verse 1, which reads, "the righteous are as bold as a lion." The verse Mark chose was Proverbs Chapter 30, Verse 30, which reads, "a lion, mighty among beasts, who retreats before nothing." We decided that the best place for this tattoo was on the left side of our chest near our heart.

The tattoo represents our individual and collective hardships. We have been scratched and scarred by the experiences and pains of our lives. Still, we *choose* to honor the purpose and meaning within those scars and the connection we have because of them. We connect to each other as father and son, as well as to God above, in every experience we encounter. I had no idea when we got our tattoos that one day seeing Mark's tattoo on his chest as he lay lifeless in a hospital bed would become a prevailing inspiration to me and others.

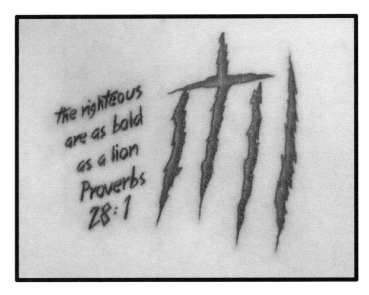

Kevin's Tattoo – Proverbs 28:1

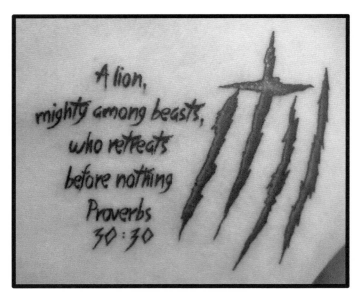

Mark's Tattoo – Proverbs 30:30

The Lion's Roar

The lion chronicles of my relationship with Mark are long and historied throughout his life, but these are my extra special memories from over the years. Hopefully, now you better understand the meaning behind the phrase I purposely used, "this young man is a lion fighting hard" from my last social media update and where we now pick up the hospital saga once again.

CHAPTER V
WRESTLING A
WAKING GATOR

Hope is not a substitute for pain. Hope is in spite of pain. Sometimes the things that hurt are worth the pain.

—Jon Foreman (Lead Singer of Switchfoot)

It was now late Tuesday night, November 12th. Mark was stirring, he had squeezed each of our hands earlier that day which filled us with new hope that he would survive at the very least, but we were a long, *long* way from anything substantial in the course of recovery.

Responding to simple commands was a great sign of brain activity, but it did not yet reflect any concrete cognitive status. The roadblocks still looming large for our son were entirely gaining back all physical and mental functions.

As the sedation continued to wear off as his body temperature climbed back to normal, the medical team warned me again that his reactions could be erratic and unpredictable. From Mark's perspective, he still had not regained full consciousness, so his body reacted like a prisoner trying to break free from chains that held it bound up.

RISE! MIRACLE THROUGH A FATHER'S EYES

As we passed the hour of midnight and into the early morning hours of Wednesday, November 13th, the episodes of my son convulsing and contorting in the hospital bed were ramping up. Now his eyelids were open when it would happen, but most times, his eyes would be rolled into the back of his head as he jerked to try and free his hands from being tied down at the side of the bed.

Each time an episode began, I would position my body over his much as I could, with my chest on his and my right arm draped over his left shoulder and arm. I would then use one or both hands to hold his head steady as I continued my mantras of prayer, quoting of scripture, and exhorts of fight into my son's right ear.

He would compete to pull his head out of my hand(s) every time; he would arch his back as if to say, "get off me," and there were groans of pain or frustration coming from his mouth in between the coughing now as well. It felt like I was wrestling a live wild gator!

I have never wrestled a gator, mind you, but after living in the south for a while, I read about and watched it on TV many times. What I saw those guys go through to wrangle a gator seemed comparable to what I was doing there in that hospital room. The difference is that one can be detached emotionally from any gator, but for me, I had to wrestle my own son.

I felt he was responding to me each time he had a convulsion episode but was I just kidding myself? As the hours wore on, I started to feel defeated inside. It was sheer misery for me to watch and feel my son writhe in such pain and confusion. I wondered if what I was doing by wrestling with him each time was making any real difference.

Wrestling a Waking Gator

Immediately following one of Mark's worst violent episodes, Mike Gatlin, one of the primary nurses caring for him, approached me at the foot of his bed and shared something I will never forget.

No doubt Mike had heard me let out that deep, vanquished sigh as I fought with my emotions right after getting Mark calmed down again from a severe outburst. He must have also perceived my feeling crushed right then when he spoke, saying, "Kevin, I want you to know that I am watching Mark's vital signs on the monitors when you wrestle with him and talk in his ear. His heart slows, and his breathing calms down *every* time. What you are doing is making a difference in the fight to bring your son back, so don't give up!"

As he spoke, I tried to process what he was saying as I looked into his eyes. You can imagine how I reacted when he finished. I acknowledged Mike, thanking him for the kind words, and told him it meant a great deal as I continued to fight back soul-level sentiment. He may or may not have known how much that truly meant to me then, but I want to clarify it now.

Single acts of courage can change the course of one life or many lives.

Those words put wings on my spirit at that moment and roused my soul with resilience. Mike, I want to thank you for being an amazing nurse and showing incredible emotional intelligence and heart to a hurting father. You identified my connection to my son and put an intrinsic value on it. That may not be in your job description, yet what you offered me in the way of hope in that instance cannot be given enough recognition or gratitude!

Single acts of courage can change the course of one life or many lives. The courage that Mike showed in his physical care and positive outlook for my son that night will go down as one of the most heroic things I have ever seen. Without his actions and timely words that altered the state of my psyche, who knows how things may have gone differently in the hours and days to follow. Mike, I love you for that man and always will!

Mark had a few more bad episodes over the next hour as he coughed and struggled; his body was trying to rid itself of the fluid that had built up in his lungs over the previous two days. Meanwhile, I had a new outlook in my spirit after Mike's words earlier, which gave me a boldness to face anything—to keep helping my son however I could, no matter what would come next. It turns out that what came next was one of the hardest things I have ever had to endure.

Feeling I needed to collect my strength after one of his episodes, I sat in the chair on the right side of his bed. As Mark became more aware and awake during his episodes, he began trying to communicate despite his lethargic state. I had only been sitting for a few minutes (watching him like a hawk) when suddenly, he pushed his chest up and leaned toward me to get my attention. I rose quickly and saw that Mark was using his left hand, still strapped to the hospital bed, making motions toward the breathing tube. He was telling me that he wanted the breathing tube out. My heart crumpled and sank in my chest.

I grabbed his hand in mine and said, "We can't take the tube out yet, son. You still need it to help you breathe." Upon hearing those words, he turned his head away from me and pushed his neck and face up toward the ceiling, beginning to cry hard. The excruciating pain in his eyes was gut-wrenching.

Wrestling a Waking Gator

He quickly looked back at me again, with massive tears streaming down his cheeks and desperation all over his face, groaning again as if to beg, "Please, help me, Dad!"

Never have I felt more sadness in my entire life than I did during those few minutes with my son. The pleading and agony he bore on his face and the way he tightly squeezed my hand was the worst torture a father could ever face. I was helpless to take this burden from my son. Worse still, I knew he could not understand why I would not help him. Even worse was being unsure if he knew who I was!

I would prefer to have my heart ripped out of my chest and beaten with a nail-ridden club rather than look at my son in this state. Even as I write these words now, I am ushered right back to that picture of his face, his suffering, his despondency, and all I can do is weep. It will forever be one of my *worst* memories and a situation I hope I never have to revisit in this life—*ever again*!

All I could do was hold his hand and tell him everything would be alright, though I did not believe my own words at the time. He finally calmed down, the sedatives finally kicked back in as his eyes rolled to the back of his head, and he fell back asleep.

I fully confess that I could no longer hold back my emotions after watching what I had just seen. I went straight to the dark back corner of the CCU room, lowered my head, covered my face with both hands, and completely broke down for the next few minutes. Thankfully, those few minutes were uninterrupted by my son or the medical staff.

At one point, I glared toward the heavens and begged God to let me trade places with him, to let me die so that my son may live—it was unbearable anguish like nothing I have felt before or since.

Strangely though, I could somehow feel God fully present in my sorrow. Despite it all, I still felt trust in my heart towards Him, which helped calm me and bring me back to the battle at hand. I used my shirt to wipe away the tears, grabbed a paper towel to blow my nose, and then returned to the chair beside my son's bed, now composed and poised for the next round.

Later that morning, after Crystal and Hannah had returned, the medical team decided to have Mark try to breathe on his own without the ventilator, in no small part because of his body language that begged to be free of it! I knew that this was yet another critical milestone; to see if his body could hold itself up without the help of machines. As the moment approached to shut it down and see how he responded, we prayed and held *our* breath.

When they flipped the switch off, I remember bracing myself to hear loud beeps from his monitors signaling that he was not responding, that he still needed the ventilator, but they never came. He was breathing on his own! He had coaching from the medical staff as the sedation meds were still pushing him in and out of consciousness, but he respired on his own for about 30 minutes before they reengaged the machine.

After successfully achieving that feat, they also tried to take him off the heavy pain medications. Sadly, he only made it about 15 minutes before acknowledging with a head nod that he was feeling intense pain and had to restart the pain meds again. Madison, the other amazing primary nurse, who had taken over for Mike after a shift change, assured us the return to pain meds was customary.

Wrestling a Waking Gator

Things had calmed a bit after about 7:30 a.m., so I retreated to the corner of the CCU room again to pen out my next update as Hannah and Crystal were attending to Mark. At around 8:00 a.m. on Wednesday, 11/13, I hit "Post" and sent my corresponding email to share the latest with the still-growing world of people following my son's saga.

Mark did pretty well throughout the night. Some rough moments around coughing and fluid on his lungs they are still trying to remove. He is now able to nod yes or no when you ask questions, on top of all the other progress he made yesterday.

The real keys for today are going to be the MRI, and they have already started the process of trying to get him off the ventilator sometime today. He was breathing without the machine on his own (with coaching as he is still pretty rummy from the meds and sedation) for about 30 mins. He was taking big deep breaths, so he was not breathing totally normally but still moving in the right direction.

He was off the meds for a while but nodded that he was feeling pain after about 15 mins, so he had to go back on. Again, that is pretty normal.

PLEASE PRAY for the MRI, the pain to subside & for him to be able to remove the ventilator tube sometime today. He really hates that thing & I know he wants it out but still needs it at the moment.

Pray also for strength for all of us. As you can imagine, we want Mark back 100%, but this process is hard and slow, and tough to watch him go through all this.

KEEP THE FAITH!!

I finished my update no sooner than the room was abuzz again, with doctors starting their morning rounds. There was always a sense of anxious anticipation and reservation each morning as we awaited the latest news and made plans for the day ahead.

The neurology team shared their plans for this day, stating the main goal was to get Mark off the breathing tube. They were pleased with the successful short-term neurology test they conducted on him when they first arrived in his room and the latest win with him off the ventilator while breathing on his own for half an hour. That, combined with the fact that he had not suffered any clinical seizures whatsoever, made them confident that we could proceed with this next step.

They had been very conservative with the timing of removing the breathing tube because it is tough for a patient to have to re-insert if there were a setback or seizure. That said, they waited to reach at least 90% assurance in their medical opinion that Mark could manage having it removed.

Despite what I had to endure at my son's side merely a few hours earlier, I was thankful for this guarded method. We all wanted to see him get his breathing tube out so we could hear his voice beating on our eardrums again. However, we all knew it was more important to approach each step of trying to bring him back with the utmost precaution.

The doctor's second goal for this day was to complete the exhaustive brain MRI. This test was to be the absolute baseline for the *actual* state of his brain function—this was the primary barrier to Mark making a full recovery.

We already had assurances from the cardiologist team that the WPW was curable *if* that was the only thing wrong with his heart. But let us be real—if Mark were unable to remember who we were or access his memories, unable to control his body for himself, unable to live life as he did before, the Mark we knew would be dead.

> **We are meant to live life to its fullest, yet death often comes to steal, kill, or destroy the most important things in our lives.**

We would sacrifice everything to keep him alive in any capacity and would *never* love him any less, of course. My point here is simply that a heart can be beating strong, yet the person we knew can be entirely gone if their mind becomes broken and inaccessible for a two-way relationship.

This severed access was our greatest fear—that Mark would lose his personality, his humor, his experiences, his future, and his ability to know his pride. It is the stuff of nightmares for anyone when thinking about someone they love. We always intend to live life to its fullest, yet too many times, death comes to steal, kill, or destroy the most important things in our lives. We did not want that for our Mark, so we vowed to keep fighting!

Throughout the morning leading up to midday, Mark continued to awaken further while making the exaggerated effort to communicate that he wanted that breathing tube out of his body for good. Finally, the time had come, which I believe was sometime right after the Noon hour. They asked us all to leave the room for the process of removing the breathing tube. A myriad of possibilities existed, from vomiting to having to re-insert the tube after a vitals crash, so they needed to be able to care for him accordingly.

Hannah, Crystal, and I took turns telling Mark what was about to happen, that we were praying for him and would be right back at his side just as soon as possible. He seemed to have a relative grasp that something imperative was about to take place, and his eyes seemed to speak that he was ready.

As we walked out to the waiting room, I recall feeling thankful that we had even reached the point of *talking* about being able to take out the breathing tube, much less see it done. I had often wondered in the previous 48 hours if I would ever see Mark without that tube or be able to talk to him again.

About 17 to 19 minutes passed, if I remember correctly, and they came out to tell us that they had successfully removed the ventilator tube, that he had done excellently, and that he was awake and trying to talk. Hearing that news thrilled all of us! We practically sprinted back to his CCU room when we were able, and there he was, sitting up at a 45-degree angle in the bed with *no breathing tube*!

His nurse, Madison, started asking him basic questions like, "Do you know who you are?" and "What is your name?" or "What year is it?" with only a tiny break in between each one. Mark answered Madison's questions correctly, albeit slowly, as each new correct answer flooded us with more aspiration than the last.

He could only respond in whispers because his throat was so raw and sore from the ventilator tube having been in since the previous Sunday. Nonetheless, to hear whispers coming out of our son's mouth while we stood witness was yet another massive miracle! He was going to survive, in as much as any of us could say for sure. This fact came as a colossal relief.

We all knew the complete MRI was still ahead of us to fully ascertain the actual level of brain damage Mark incurred from the oxygen deprivation, but I do not think any of us cared at that moment. My son gave us all we needed right then with his retorts and efforts to show he was fighting to reconnect to life.

The team of neurologists was back a brief time later and began their full inquiry of him. They asked a battery of questions addressing his motor skills—requesting that he move his fingers and toes, lift his arms and legs, and move his head up or down or side to side. Incredibly, Mark successfully reacted to each command!

In between their questions, Mark began to ask his own, with the first and primary question being, "Can I have water?" That query came because he felt super thirsty after ditching the throat cylinder that had been choking him for days. They told him he could have ice chips, so we began to feed him those as they continued their interrogation.

They moved from motor skill questions to people identification, and while he could recognize faces and positively nod when asked if he knew someone in the room, he could not remember our names. We were assured that this was very normal, but at the time, it was a blunt reminder that we had a long way to go. We were not focused on that at all, however. We were only ecstatic at his progress and our being able to talk to Mark out loud once again!

The doctors completed their analysis, stating they were pleased and even more optimistic now with how well he was doing. They encouraged us to ask questions occasionally to check his memory but to do so reassuringly without getting frustrated if he could not remember. After that, since they were still waiting on a confirmation of an official time for his MRI, they pledged to come back later to check on him.

Once the medical staff had gone from the room, I just wanted to stand next to my son. I moved to the right side of the bed, kept putting my hand on his head or shoulder, and told him how much I loved him and how good it was to see him fully awake, talking, and moving on command. His eyes were as blue as I had ever remembered them being, yet still vacant most of the time as he struggled to access memories and fought with the drugs still coursing through his veins, making him extremely drowsy.

I stepped away after a while to watch Hannah and Crystal as they interacted with him. It did my heart good to see these women no longer devastated by anguish but now overflowing with smiles just being with Mark.

An hour or so passed when the medical team returned shortly after 2:00 p.m. to reassess my son. They revved up the necessary interrogation once again. While he did pretty well with most of their unintimidating gentle probing over the next 15 to 20 minutes, it was apparent—he could not remember details or specifics. He knew his dog Kovu by a picture Hannah showed him and even smiled a bit. He kissed Hannah and told her he missed her. But the fact remained that Mark could not muster identities by name when the medical team or any of us asked. Mark's merely attempting to answer questions at this stage, even if he was highly hazy, was so encouraging after being in a total coma merely 24 hours before.

With it now being apparent to all that he was going to survive, they shared that their new plan was to be able to send Mark home sometime by or before Christmas, depending on how his recovery and rehabilitation progressed in the coming weeks. Given all that he had been through and the fact that he was *well* ahead of any planned recovery schedule they had given us initially, they decided to postpone the exhaustive brain MRI until the following morning. They told us to be patient, let things come naturally, and we would see what the next day would bring.

Seeing the smiles and joy on the faces of the medical team while they quizzed Mark and spoke to us was special because we knew that all too often, they had to cope with patients spiraling downward and even dying. The upward projection of my son was a welcome turnabout for all of them. We again thanked each doctor, and then they left for the evening.

Elated at the day's events, I knew the outside world would want to share in this fantastic new progress. This time, I retreated to the waiting room to give Hannah and Crystal alone time with Mark and get a moment to myself. I paused *everything* for a few minutes, sitting in the waiting room alone, forcing myself through deep, slow-breathing exercises.

It felt so good to inhale the good news of the day and exhale the anxieties and fears that had attached to me over the last two days like dirty little leeches. I picked up my smartphone around

4:00 p.m. on Wednesday, 11/13, to script the latest social media blast and email update. Hitting "Post" this time came with an emphatic finger blast to the screen, a minor physical proclamation of the fist-pumping exhilaration I felt inside.

Mark is off the breathing tube entirely, talking softly; he knows his dog Kovu and smiled at a picture of him, he knows our faces, and he told Hannah he missed her and kissed her on the cheek and has been begging for water ever since the tube came out! He can move all his fingers and toes on command.

People, Jesus conquered death in 3 days, and he has chosen to walk our son back to us in just 3 days' time as well!

JESUS IS KING!!! POWERFUL & MIGHTY TO SAVE!!

It was you, family, all over North America, in Africa, and God knows where else who joined us in prayer, and we are forever in your debt!!
We are not completely out of the woods just yet; he is still struggling with names and memories, so he will be doing an MRI likely tomorrow now, followed by a Coronary Artery procedure to check to see if he has any artery issues due to his T1D.

The Docs don't think that is the case but want to be safe and check. Then the final procedure will be to fix the "false electrical paths" growing on his heart, diagnosed as the Wolff Parkinson White syndrome. That procedure will take 60 to 90 minutes and likely will take place on either Friday or Monday, depending on the other progression steps he needs to have completed before that final procedure.

Thank you from the bottom of our heart to all of you who have prayed, and please continue for a 100% recovery, particularly for his heart and memories now. And thanks be to Jesus for your mercy, grace, and healing and for allowing us to keep our Mark here in this life.

KEEP THE FAITH!! It is powerful beyond belief!
There just are no words beyond that!

Once I had sent it, I made myself re-read it several times to soak it all in. I was so tired, yet with my son alive, I felt like I could have taken on the whole world at once! I was also astonished at all the encouragement and prayer being shot back to me for my son from literally all over the world.

One of our closest friends Spirit Laursen, whom we had raised our kids with together for so many years when we lived in North Idaho at the same time, sent us something I will cherish forever. She sent an email earlier this very day, just before I had sent out the update you read on the previous page, which contained a video from where her missionary husband Erik was ministering in Africa.

The video was a 6-minute prayer from about 17 to 20 people—strangers to us—who were all interceding for our son in prayer, speaking simultaneously. As Crystal and I watched the video, all we could do was cry, blown away that on another continent, there were people who did not know us in the slightest, who were willing to take time to pray so hard and long for our son.

Those prayers and the prayers of so many others across the globe were fuel for my soul. They filled me up again each time my faith tank ran dry from all I was facing in that room with Mark. Without those prayers, I doubt I would have been able to wrestle that waking gator. Man, oh man, did I wrestle that gator! I would not discover for months what those wrestling matches physically wrought upon me. Yet, looking back, I would do it again in a heartbeat because I was *father* to this gator struggling to wake up—and a waking gator is a *LIVE* gator!

CHAPTER VI
WAR OF WHO & WHY

Faith is an organ of knowledge,
and love an organ of experience.

—A.W. Tozer

Released from the machine that had been in control of his lungs, my son was involuntarily enlisted in a new war; the war of who and why. He was answering well the fundamental questions of where, what, and when, yet he unmistakably had holes in his brainwaves. Those holes did not allow him to connect to who and why on even simple levels, much less the deeper memories of his life. He was interacting with us, moving in and out of consciousness, yet distant and woozy most of the time. I would just sit for long periods by his side, as would my wife and Hannah, just to watch him breathe.

Watching his lungs work on their own without the help of any artificial contraption was so inspiring. Crazy that something we take for granted so readily, like lungs pumping life-giving air in and out of our body, can become so important instantly.

Mark would often wake with a startle looking over at whoever was sitting next to him—you could tell by looking into his eyes that he was trying to make things work in his brain. The eyes are a two-way mirror into our soul, transparently revealing what is occurring within our spirit and emotions no matter what picture we *think* we are portraying from the inside out. Looking into my son's eyes, it was evident that a deep search heavily taxed his entire being.

> **The eyes are a two-way mirror into our soul, transparently revealing what is occurring within our spirit and emotions no matter what picture we *think* we are portraying from the inside out.**

Growing up, I taught him that making eye contact was crucial for meaningfully relating to people, so he was reverting to that instinctually as he tried to piece together what was happening to him. You could hear the questions bubbling within his brain without uttering a word. Why am I in this hospital bed? Why is it hard for me to speak? I think I know this person sitting next to me—I recognize their face, but why am I struggling to remember who they are?

Each of us, when we sat with him, would remind him occasionally where he was, why he was there, who he was, and reassure him of who we were. His eyes seemed to process peace with those reminders most of the time. Then again, there were also those moments when he would turn his head away, almost as if to say, "I can't remember what I think I should be able to, which hurts too much." That was exceedingly hard for all of us to watch.

Fear flashed now and then in his eyes, revealing the uncertainty he felt about himself and life as he knew it. It struck such a stark contrast from his usual confidence and assuredness before the accident. It made me pause again to ponder in my mind whether the damage to his brain would rob him of specific memories and capabilities forever. The reality was we were all battling our brains now, burdened by the veiled future that still lay ahead.

Madison came in often to check on Mark, and I remember how much I appreciated her sincere smile and strong spirit. She conveyed she cared about him and us without ever having to speak the words—the truest indication of an excellent nurse! My son did not know her at all, yet he has always been a good judge of character. One could see by how Mark responded to her that he trusted she was there to help and indeed cared about him.

> **Do not underestimate your influence on a person when you are trying to help them out of the darkness—the light you shine from right where you are is a guide from the peril of a sinking death to the anchor of a rescued life.**

He was progressing with each passing minute and seemed so calm that Madison made the call that we could remove the wrist restraints. That felt like his being released from prison for both him and us too!

Almost immediately, he began to use his arms to inspect himself—likely both consciously and unconsciously—to ascertain what he felt in particular places on his arms, legs, and head. Undoubtedly, he was questioning the absence of context, which would typically be present with such a probing of pains or mysteries on or in his own body.

The temple on the left side of his head was the primary point of inspection due to the large gash he suffered from falling. He would reach up, carefully feel around it, and then look to whoever was next to him for an explanation. We explained the injury each time he would touch it; then, he would move on to survey the rest of his head.

It is both fascinating and disturbing to watch someone connect links from what they are feeling to facts when there are apparent gaps in the timeline of their memory. Mark could feel pain from the various injuries down the left side of his body yet could not remember how they got there. That void in his reminiscence resulted in a routine bodily inspection and a corresponding inquisition to whoever was beside him at the time. However, it would be a while before his brain could accept the explanation because the memory was not there. Like a train conductor approaching a blown-out bridge, his mind had to stop each time because tracks once present were now replaced by an abyss that kept him from getting to the other side.

That would be a trip, wouldn't it? To have injuries on your own body without recollecting how they got there? I often think about what images were going through his mind when he could not yet fully remember the who or why. It would cause such a kaleidoscope of confusion in one's brain—trying so painstakingly to remember yet having to rely on information from outside your own mind, from people you do not recognize fully, to fill those many gaps. I felt compassion for my son and wished again that there were more I could do to curb his confusion.

I must make a declaration here, though—do not underestimate your influence on a person when you are trying to help them out of the darkness. This person may not see or know you readily, but one cannot logically explain the recognition that is present; the assurance they sense and the light they feel becomes a force that successfully guides their recovery.

Accepting the role of guide to someone in this state is preposterously hard; at times, you will feel you are not making any difference but stay the course. Imagine yourself as a lighthouse on the ocean shoreline—you may not be able to see or reach the ship trapped out in the dark raging grip of an angry ocean storm, but the light you shine from right where you are is a guide from the peril of a sinking death to the anchor of a rescued life.

One thing helping Mark was physical touch. There is an excellent book, *The Five Love Languages,* by Gary Chapman, in which he describes five "languages" by which we receive love as human beings: acts of service, receiving gifts, quality time, words of affirmation, and physical touch. If you have not read it, I highly recommend it as it is an excellent tool for interacting with all the people closest in our lives.

Chapman describes in his book that while we need all *five* love languages, we have *two* that are *primary* in how we most readily receive love from others. Mark and I always shared physical touch as one of our primary love languages.

From the time he was a little boy, the kid just did not understand what was happening around him until the activity involved some form of physical touch. For example, as a toddler, he would get overcharged and go tearing through the house, and I would have to reach out and clothesline him like a pro-wrestler—knocking him down (not too roughly, Mom, he was always fine) and then jumping on top of him to get his attention.

He would look up at me with that shocked look of "what is going on?" while I explained that he was out of control. Mark and I would end up hysterically laughing as I worked to send the message to him of "CALM DOWN!" It still makes me laugh today to think about it.

Energizer bunny? That bunny has nothing on my kid as a human pinball! I am seriously laughing aloud again right now—I had way too much fun with him when he was little.

God knew when I was getting ready to become a father that I worried about the whole baby thing. I was terrified I would break a baby with how fragile they are—so God sent me Mark as my first born. That kid was freakishly indestructible!

Don't believe me? All right, let me share another quick anecdote to prove my point. At three years old, I remember Mark purposefully running from the couch directly into our entertainment center—on purpose, mind you. I was sitting behind him and flinched hard with a screwed-up look on my face thinking to myself, "man, that must have hurt," while I waited for him to start wailing. But he did not.

In fact, he came back to the couch, grabbed a big fat pillow, then turned around only to run himself back into the entertainment center even harder! He fell backward to the ground and busted out with belly roll laughter that made me uproariously laugh so hard I was crying for the next 15 minutes. That was Mark—he would do anything for a laugh and was fearless of bodily harm, to a detriment at times.

It always took a form of physical touch to reach him. Any time he was hurt or mad, from toddler to teenager, all I had to do was put my hand on his back, shoulder, or head to ramp him down (most of the time anyway—wink). That fact was now a weapon we all would use against the fear he felt as he lay there in the hospital bed as a young 21-year-old man. Every time we spoke to him, we held his hand or put our hand on his head or shoulder. We could sense it put Mark more at ease, even though he could not understand the sights or sounds of his situation.

As late afternoon faded off and gave way to early evening, the fatigue and hunger set in for everyone again, so Crystal and Hannah left to get a meal and a reprieve from all the heavy happenings of the day. As I stood alone again next to Mark, I sensed this night was going to be different. He could speak now, so his ability to communicate what he was feeling from his perspective was going to make everything infinitely easier when it came to caring for him. I was beyond thankful for that—because it had been the stuff of nightmares not to hear him tell me what he was experiencing for himself.

When nightmares compound in a situation like ours, it is difficult to put one challenging thing above another. Still, one of the hardest things for me—a hell in all reality—was watching Mark strain to remember his people gathered around him as he crawled out of his coma. He did not *know his pride*. Gazing into someone's eyes only to see blank incapability of full recognition looking back at you from a person you have shared any length of time with, much less 21 years, is insanely painful and frightening.

The chief neurologist had explained to all of us, as you recall from when he was in the CCU room earlier that day, that we needed to begin unobtrusively probing Mark's memory. Our goal was to ascertain how much was "lost" currently and help him find his way back to his memories if possible. He warned us not to push too hard or aggravate him about what he could not remember because each memory that Mark could not recall would frustrate him and stir up anxiety which would be detrimental to his mental recovery.

I felt so uneasy inside with this challenge from the doctor—the charge to walk a fine line of helping and not hurting. The cautious yet courageous approach with a prominence of patience it would require would be wildly tough. When you want so badly for someone to return to what they once knew for themself and you, it is difficult for anyone not to push harder than one should, it is even harder for someone as driven as I am!

With a nervousness I had never experienced, I accepted the challenge of beginning my quest into Mark's mind. The hope, of course, was that he would rediscover wide recognition and that all of us could be witnesses to him reconnecting with his distant and near memories.

To combat my nerves, I produced a plan—to watch my son's body language, look into his eyes for signs of awareness every 10 to 12 minutes, then naturally and unassumingly ask him an easy question.

I took my first stab at it when I saw Mark seemingly more coherent than he had been during the day. Gathering myself, trying to keep any expectation out of my mind, I rolled the words from brain to tongue and asked him a simple short question.

"Hey, Mark, who am I, pal?"

I asked playfully with a smile strapped on my face, almost like it was a game. Then, I leaned in close as he turned his head toward me so that I would hear his whisper talk—I could see the wheels turning in his mind.

Staring me down, he quietly answered.

"Chaplain," he said, tilting his head as if waiting for me to confirm that he gave the correct answer.

"Alright, I'll take that, buddy. I have been praying over you a lot," I said.

I was thinking that his neurons, while trying to collect themselves during his coma, were likely recalling all the prayers I had been speaking nonstop into his ears. His answer of "Chaplain" meant that perhaps he did experience a connection in his mind between my voice and what his ears heard unconsciously during recent days. I clung to that small nugget of hope.

Something I found bizarre was only to hear whispers coming out of my son—because if you know Mark, you know he is one of the loudest people on the face of the planet. I am convinced that when God was forming this kid in his mother's womb, he decided to put every sound, of every living thing, into this *single* human being. His inability to tap into this vast library of noise within was in and of itself a statement that Mark was not yet able to find or be his true self.

I sat back in the chair next to his bed and waited for my next opportunity to delve into my son's mind. After 8 or 9 minutes, Mark motioned me over to his bed and asked for more ice chips because he was still thirsty.

This action gave me another chance, so I asked him that same question again with a different language twist.

"Mark, who am I, buddy?"

He stared at me hard again, chewing his ice chips vigorously like a cow chewing grass in the field. I could see him trying hard to remember. Then after completing his chew and swallowing, he responded by saying, "Pastor."

Chuckling aloud, I said back to him, "True, I have been talking a whole lot of Bible into your ears over the last few days for sure, bud."

The look on his face suggested a satisfaction that I had affirmed to him his answer was acceptable and accurate. Then, he turned his head away from me and closed his eyes, returning to the safety of impeding his eyes from bringing forth any other senseless images.

This time, when he turned away, I felt a sting inside, like a colossal bee had somehow crawled into my chest cavity and plunged its painful stinger right into my heart. I wanted so badly to see the fact of my being his father return to his vacant eyes. I could feel the venom from that stinger in my heart pulsating— taunting that my *own son* did not know me.

Another 10 or 11 minutes passed, and he was stirring again. I got up from the chair to ask a third time, this time with a hook of who he was to me that I thought may provoke a pang of identity back from him.

"Mark, who am I, son?"

This time his answer came very quickly, with a deviant little smirk in the corner of his mouth as he fired out in a loud whisper.

"Jimmy!"

"Jimmy?!" I exclaimed in return as I pulled back my head with a screwed-up face, raised my left eyebrow, then countered laughingly.

"You mean like Jimmy John's? You hungry for a sandwich or something, pal?"

That made him break out in a cheeky grin, as he laughed under his breath and turned his head back to the other side of the room. I could not tell at that point if he was joking with me and knew who I was or if he was genuinely struggling to put a name to my face. Mark has always been a jokester, remember, so that smirk on his face when he answered left me unsure one way or the other.

As another 11 or 12 minutes clicked away on the universe's clock, I could not belay the anxiousness inside of me, so I figured I would try one last time before calling it quits on inquiries for the night.

I leaned over the bed this time, got right up in his grill, then quipped with half-squinted eyes, "Alright, buddy, who am I?"

Mark responded immediately and emphatically with a twinkle in his big blue eyes.

"Enrique," he cracked, followed by a breathy laugh.

I jerked my head back, dropped my mouth open, and snapped back.

"Enrique?!" I barked loudly and sarcastically.

"Do I look like an Enrique to you?"

I paused for effect, then followed up with, "Seriously?!"

Mark was fully wheeze-laughing now, looking back and forth from me to the ceiling. He had to have been pulling my chain, right? Yet he did not follow up with any other answer. That made me laugh and scared me at the same time. What if my son truly did not know who I was?

I promptly passed that unimaginable thought out of my head and got back in his face. I said, "Oh yeah, you love being the funny man, don't you," as I stuffed some more ice in his pie hole—with him continuing his wheezy glee like Ed, the hyena with crazy eyes from *The Lion King* who never talked but only laughed.

Setting the glass of ice chips down on his tray table, I slumped defeatedly back into the chair next to his bed. I so loved seeing him laughing and lighthearted again, but I desperately wanted him to be serious, to tell me who I was to him. Then again, perhaps in that last hour, or even the previous few days for that matter, I *was* all those things to him.

Maybe I was "Chaplain" or "Pastor" because he needed me to bring a spirituality he would have recognized from his years of growing up around me, his mom, and so many other people of faith.

Perhaps I was "Jimmy" or "Enrique" for no reason other than maybe he needed to exercise his humor with me again. I did not know, but I closed my eyes to say another prayer that my son would come to know me once again.

It is a remarkable gift to *know* someone—to recognize them fully and recall your rich history with them. To relive the experiences and connections you have shared with this person over so many years is an unparalleled prize; to understand their tendencies, desires, and pains and have them understand yours in return. I wanted desperately for all that to come rushing back to Mark when he thought of me.

> **It is a remarkable gift to *know* someone—to recognize them fully and recall your rich history with them.**

Sitting in the chair feeling forlorn, almost drifting off for about 7 or 8 minutes in the rare, brief quiet that had overtaken his room, I was startled by Mark waving his arm and motioning me back to the bed. I rose out of the chair and leaned my head down toward his face to hear those whispers when out of his mouth came, "Dad, can you get me some more ice chips?"

It was as if the world stopped entirely as soon as the word "Dad" reached my ear drums. Not since the first time he called me "Da-Da" when he was a tiny toddler have I ever been so delighted to hear him recognize me as his dad! I felt a rush of reprieve sweep over me from head to toe. That made not just my day but my whole life. I knew that if he still recognized me as his dad in any capacity in his mind, we would be able to share more father-to-son experiences in this life.

> **When a word is fathomless with story, it cannot be overstated how much meaning can inhabit that single word.**

I put my hand on his forehead and answered back, with the most oversized look of joy and affirmation I could muster stretched all over my face.

"Son, I will absolutely get you more ice chips, and it is *so* good to hear the word 'Dad' come out of your mouth!"

My heart was pounding out of my chest with exhilaration, over just *one* word. When a word is fathomless with story, one cannot overstate how much meaning can inhabit that single word.

Our father-to-son journey was yet unfinished, so getting this reassurance that our story would continue in any form was enough for me, leaving me grateful beyond words.

When Crystal returned to the room, I shared with her the "Who am I?" game that had taken place while she was out. She both laughed and shared in the obvious emotion that he had called me dad. I held her in a huge bear hug, and she knew what I was feeling without having to say anything more.

My wife had watched me be a dad to Mark for over two decades and fully understood what being a father to him, and his brother meant to me. She could feel in my hug what I could not put into words right then—how happy I was to still be a dad to a living son there in that hospital room.

Together we spent a bit of time taking turns sitting by his side or attending to him as needed, and it felt so good to be sharing time with our son—watching him, talking to him, just being in his presence. We rotated out after that to get a break, make phone calls, grab food, and give Hannah time alone with Mark.

I remember the food I ate that night seemed to have taste, which I had neither the time nor interest in with any of the food I had consumed over the last few days. What I was eating tasted *good,* surprisingly. It was the first time I was conscious of anything beyond the trauma, my first awareness of something "normal" since Mark had collapsed. The taste of good food brought with it a simple prospect that life still yearned to bring good things to me, to us. My heart had been previously incapable of engaging with that concept, which was a symbolic shift in my life stance.

I spent some time outside the hospital and forced myself into deep breathing again after I had finished eating. Consciously, with every inhale, I focused on taking in faith, hope, love, and all things good; with every exhale, I focused on letting go of every fear, pain, doubt, and all bad things still entombed within me. I felt the scintillating spirit of "RISE!"

The dictionary defines "rise" with two meanings. The first is "move from a lower position to a higher one." The second is "get up from lying, sitting, or kneeling." I felt both of those meanings now merging inside.

Though death lingered still, repulsively breathing its putrid vapors of hopelessness and suffering onto the back of my neck even now, a recoil deep in my soul responded and defiantly blew back against those vile fumes. A definitive "RISE!" was forming and gaining strength within me.

> **Inhale faith, hope, and love. Exhale fear, pain, and doubt. Feel the scintillating spirit of *RISE* surge within your soul.**

As I finished my intentional breathing, the defiance surging in me pushed my thoughts to a song called "Look What You've Done" by one of my favorite rock trios, Tree 63. With the words from the chorus of that song ringing in my ears, I purposefully directed my thoughts to look at what God had done in just a few short days. My son was dead and gone on Sunday night—yet now he was awake and had called me Dad.

I had just been through the worst 72-hour period of my life, yet the vision that came to my mind as I stared up into a starry South Carolina sky was a welcome one. After days of descending, being dragged down, and left paralyzed there at the lowest point of the valley of the shadow of death, I suddenly sensed that I was no longer incapacitated. I was slowly stepping forward, in heavy fog still but now on the slightest incline, which my body and spirit eagerly absorbed as the change of direction I desperately longed for—up.

With each wary step, my eyes which had been blind could now see the faint form of light in the distance through the thick fog. I hastily glanced back down at the decline and darkness that had pulled me down and held me immobile over these last days, but something was different now, "RISE!" was calling me from beyond. I knew there was a long ascent still ahead; nonetheless, I felt ready to exert whatever energy necessary for the climb out of this valley and out of the clutches of death.

Yes, I have quite the active artistry that appears in my mind when I am awake and also while I am sleeping. I would not have it any other way. As God created the heavens, the earth, and all living things, is it really that hard to believe that He could brush breathtaking portraits of life's meaning within the beautiful minds of his most cherished creations?

Glorious rabbit trail—check. Now, to continue with the story.

I spent a few more minutes outside under the stars. I then returned to the CCU room to spend the night by Mark's side again so that the women in my life could get some much-needed sleep and rest after another day of riding this precarious emotional roller coaster.

Back in the chair next to his bed, I wondered what new unforeseen experiences waited on the horizon of this night. Mark's unquenchable thirst since removing the ventilator led to crazy consumption of ice chips, as that is all they would let him put in his body primarily to ensure he could adequately swallow.

Again, such routine bodily functions we usually are not even conscious of having to be re-learned and practiced after a trauma gave me pause to appreciate *my* ability to eat and drink.

Receiving all that water into his body made Mark feel like he needed to use the restroom more frequently. He would lean over and say, "I need to pee," without realizing that was already happening. The first time he asked, I calmly explained that he had a catheter to take care of that. However, understanding that involuntary medical tool was just not in the cards for him.

About every 20 to 25 minutes, or after being fed a couple of rounds of ice chips, he would call me over and whisper, "I need to go to the bathroom," yet again. After a few times of trying to explain the catheter to no avail and getting the deer-in-headlights look from him, I decided to use my humor to try and help.

"You have to pee? Just go, man!"

The reference, of course, is to how Harry had said the same to Lloyd when he had to pee in the movie *Dumb and Dumber* as they were frozen together on the moped while headed to Aspen. A smile cracked from the corners of his mouth as he apparently recognized that reference—having laughed about it many times before.

I knew he still did not understand his not needing to get up to use the restroom, which was right there in the corner of his CCU room, but he did not press the issue for a couple of hours after that as he was dipping in and out of consciousness, so I thought maybe he had let it go. Think again.

At about 3:00 a.m. on Thursday, November 14th, I had managed to dose off in the chair I had pulled up right next to his bed. I had been out only for a few minutes when I was startled and awoke to the sight of my son standing next to his hospital bed, getting ready to unhook all the monitor wires from his arms and rip the catheter out of his body!

I jumped out of my chair and yelled, "Mark, what are you doing, bud? Don't pull on any of those wires, son!"

He looked alarmed and then answered in a gruff whisper yell, "I have to pee really bad, so I'm going to the bathroom!"

I had quickly made my way over to the other side of the bed and stopped him from yanking out wires and tubes from his body, and declared this time, "Bud, your pee is on auto pilot, so don't even think about it anymore and get back in bed you nut!"

Again, he smiled at me, not completely understanding why he could not go into the restroom right next to his bed and, I guess, trusting that his dad knew what he was doing. I carefully got him back in bed and double-checked his tubes and wires for disconnections. Right after that, Madison came back in, requiring that I explain what had just happened, and we had a good laugh about it—with Mark finding joy in the fact that he had made us laugh.

Madison looked at him and said, "Alright, mister, no more trying to get out of this bed. If you need something or have a question, ask your dad, or push the button to call me, Ok?"

She went on and jokingly quipped, "Don't make me have to put those straps back on you to keep you in bed, Mark!"

Mark smiled hugely with mischief all over his face like he had so many times throughout his life and then nodded while whispering, "Ok."

That was the end of my trying to sneak in any sleep the rest of the night! I must admit I felt a little proud of the strength and initiative he had just shown to get out of bed by himself to try and get over to the restroom. Even that was a blessing to see him stand when I had wondered if he would ever again—of course, taking place rebelliously on his terms before he was supposed to even be standing.

The remainder of the night went without any more noteworthy events, with Mark getting in periodic sleep while I rested and continued to pray in the reclining chair next to his bed. We both took solace in the break from the war of who and why which both he and we had been waging all day.

CHAPTER VII
MONUMENT
OF MIRACLE

Seek not to understand that you may believe,
but believe that you may understand.

—Saint Augustine

As the early morning blackened hours of Thursday, November 14th, succumbed to the pressing light of a new day, I knew this day would be monumental. The brain MRI was on the schedule for mid-morning, and as I sat in the chair in that frigid CCU room, I had just one word bounding in the back of my brain—miracle!

I felt so conflicted within. I frantically wanted a miracle of a wholly mended mind for my son more than anything I have ever wanted. Yet, I felt highly unworthy to even remotely entertain such a radical outcome from a patient described as "too far gone" just days before. Like a hound chasing the sly fox, I dared to begin hunting this elusive miracle in my thoughts and prayers.

Just past 7:00 a.m., Crystal and Hannah returned to Mark's bedside. It was again so good to see the interaction between them, albeit scattered and woozy from Mark at times. Now he knew who they were as well, so just having his eyes open, hearing his raspy whisper voice, and seeing him smile was the morning medicine we all needed as his family. Crystal had a similar feeling as I did when she heard her son recognize her as "mom" once again—it became like a second birth for her in the relationship with her oldest child.

Hope was much more present in the air than it had been just a day earlier, yet we all knew the major milestone of facing the results of his clinical brain MRI was now imminent. Even though we did not completely understand the physical state of his heart yet, the feeling of everyone (including the doctors) was strangely optimistic on that front. The status of his brain function weighed heavily as our single most significant concern.

> **Like a hound chasing the sly fox,**
> **we should always dare to hunt**
> **the elusive miracle in our**
> **thoughts and prayers.**

The mind is such a fragile thing. What would the scan of Mark's brain reveal? We were cautiously optimistic, given the good news we had received after his initial brainwave scan (EEG) and the welcome fact that he was achieving slight recognition of certain people. However, we were also apprehensive about what a conclusive MRI may reveal.

The neurology team came in later that morning and said they would be prepping him for his MRI. It did not take them long to prepare him, and before we knew it, they were rolling his bed out of the CCU and toward a different section of the hospital to commence the brain scan.

Monument of Miracle

As I sat and waited, my prayers were specific—that the scan would find both fact and falsehood. I wanted fact; to know what my son's brain had suffered and what we could expect going forward for him and us exactly. I also wanted falsehood; to discover the prognosis that "my son's mind was too far gone" was 100% untrue.

The process did not take as long as I thought it would, or maybe it was just that I lost track of time during my prayers before they wheeled him back into the CCU. They stated they would be back later to provide the results once the chief neurologist had a chance to examine his scan thoroughly.

Those next hours in Mark's room were mercilessly brutal. We waited with uneasiness rattling in our heads and nervousness pinballing in our hearts—the unknown can be such a torturous captor. We all worked to inhale faith and exhale our fears yet again as the minutes ticked away with reality racing toward us recklessly.

Crystal and I talked at length about possible outcomes and the change Mark might face if the MRI results revealed any lasting effects or new impediments. As a parent, these are the dreaded conversations, and being forced to entertain them was more painful than we could have imagined.

We calmly weaved our way through each other's questions and concerns while consoling each other and promising to do whatever we must for our son and daughter-in-law in the future. The battle still was not just taking place in Mark's brain but within all our brains. I reminded Crystal of how far our son had come over just a few short days and highlighted the positive prospects that no longer seemed out of reach.

As we finished our conversations and embraces, time seemed to turn up the volume on the slowly moving hands of that universal ticking clock again. It was agonizing to wait out each minute for this news to make its way to us. I joked at one point that perhaps they had employed The Pony Express to deliver the message, and one of the ponies must have passed out or some other ridiculous excuse!

Finally, the medical team arrived, huddling in our room for an assessment of Mark and to reveal the results for which we had been so nervously waiting. As the chief neurologist began to speak, I could not read him. His body language did not give a hint or clue. I felt myself starting to cringe on the inside—as if I anticipated a wild animal crashing into my body in a bloody attack.

Each word from the doctor seemed to come out slower than the next, like slurred speech in a slow-motion scene of a movie. But it happened at last—he finally spit out the words, "Mark's MRI showed only *MILD* brain damage!" He went on to explain how shocked he was at this result, but the facts were there was nothing in his MRI that made him believe that my son could not make a full recovery with time and rehabilitation efforts.

Upon hearing those words while I stood right next to Mark, I leaned back, brought both hands up to my face, then raised them to rest on the top of my head. I quietly whispered, "Thank you, Jesus," under my breath as he continued his explanation.

He shared an analogy to help us wrap our minds around what had taken place in my son's brain when he went through oxygen deprivation. He said, "Think of the brain as a system of bridges which allow for safe passage of information from one area of the brain to another. When the brain is oxygen-deprived, it is as if C-4 had been strapped to each bridge then detonated, exploding them into pieces one by one."

He continued, "The longer the brain is deprived of oxygen—the more bridges are blown up. The good news is that the brain has many bridges in and out of each section, so with him having only mild brain damage, there is a good chance that his brain will re-map itself over time. He should regain most, if not all, of his long-term memories and most of his short-term memory—the only exception being the accident itself, his time in the ER, and the days he spent in and coming out of the coma. Those memories may never return."

> **The light of life waits on the other side of the thick fog, which fiendishly fashions the valley of death.**

I could not hold back my smile any longer, and I shook my head in disbelief probably 3 or 4 separate times as he spoke. I listened intently as the doctor finished by stating Mark's recovery would require rehabilitation and that there was no specific timetable he could put on a full recovery. Citing that everyone is different, he noted that overall recovery time would depend on Mark and his determination. That made me snicker a little inside because I knew my son—when he set his mind to something, only God himself could stop him.

I felt so liberated, like the wooly mammoth painfully parked firmly on the middle of my chest, finally picked up his big furry butt, and strolled away in search of some other sitting stool! I could breathe again. I could finally believe that the light I saw in my vision from earlier was not a locomotive coming to crush me onto the tracks beneath its wheels. Instead, I could sense it was the light of life waiting on the other side of the fog when we finished our walk up and out of this valley of death for good.

When the doctor finished, he turned his attention to quizzing Mark in a thorough assessment. He asked him a slew of questions, of which Mark could answer about 80% correctly. After he finished, he turned to us and said, "Your son is a miracle and well on his way to recovery. Be patient and give him time, but he is doing incredibly well! I wish him and all of you the very best because our neurological treatment is finished for now."

I shook his hand and thanked both him and his team profusely. He acknowledged us with heartfelt congratulations on his way out the door, stating that the cardiac team would be up shortly to provide the latest information and next steps to address his heart condition.

When they left the room, I threw my arms around my wife and held her so tight. Our boy was alive—his brain had survived an unconscionable accident, and only God knows how long without oxygen. I remember whispering in her ear, "Our son is still here, and God is not done with this kid of ours!"

I could feel the relief in my wife's embrace as we just held each other and cried tears of joy. I was so thankful that she would not have to endure the loss of her oldest son. His status had definitively changed; death lost its ghastly grip on our son for the moment, and the road to recovery was now in full view.

The atmosphere in that room was now thick with our gladness and renewed strength. We talked with Mark, reassuring him that his memories would return in time, emphasizing the excellent news we had just received. We knew he would not fully be able to grasp it just yet, but we kept saying it anyway to pry its blessing into his mind subliminally if nothing else.

An hour or so passed, and the cardiology team arrived in the room to assess Mark and to convey more details from the original EKG and x-ray scans along with their plans to address the WPW syndrome. They explained the state of his heart and the tests they were targeting to conduct the following day, including a cardiac MRI to check all his major arteries for any damage.

The feeling was still strong with the chief cardiologist that there had to be something more wrong than just WPW syndrome for Mark to have experienced such a catastrophic cardiac response. Yet he remained vocally optimistic as well, given how Mark had come out of the coma without significant setbacks and how rapidly he was progressing.

The team was only in the room for about 15 to 20 mins, expressing their happiness about the great results of Mark's brain MRI, then stating they would be back the following morning to reassess. At that time, they would make solid plans for the necessary tests and the eventual ablation surgery to directly address the WPW that had started all this mess in the first place. Lastly, they cleared him to have visitors in his room that afternoon, which was more welcome news to all of us.

A little after 3:00 p.m., Mark's little brother made his way into the room. It was a big moment for Brian—who, in quiet strength, had been taking care of a rambunctious pup for days and holding his mom and me together in loving support, all while managing his own fear of losing his best friend. He would finally get to see his big brother.

As a father, I could never forget the second he came in and locked eyes with Mark, which led to gigantic grins on both their faces. I teared up behind my smartphone as I got ready to snap a picture. Seeing my two sons together again, realizing they would have future moments with each other, was a special moment.

As Brian reached the side of his bed, Mark would provide a memory of hilarity for the ages as he looked at his brother and proceeded to yell-whisper, "Wow, you look like sh#@!"

Ahh, what the cocktail mix of drugs, sleep deprivation, insane trauma, and healthy humor will do to what comes out of someone's mouth, right?! We were all shocked and busted a gut laughing as Brian quickly quipped right back with, "Woah, you're one to talk, Mark!"

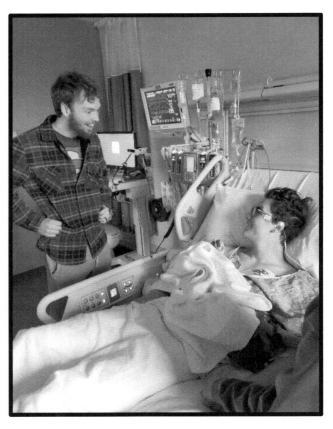

Brian visiting his older brother
in the CCU Room on Thursday, 11/14

Monument of Miracle

Mark could not even call his brother by name yet, but seeing his face ignited immediately the connection to a past in which he had always been able to say something which would make his little brother laugh. Crystal and I had witnessed those types of hysterical interactions for years, and it brought back keen flashbacks, as I had watched the two of them laugh both at and with each other to the point of hardly being able to breathe so many times.

Right then, a particular memory smashed its way into my head. When Mark was four years old, and Brian was two, they played together near our bedroom door when Mark decided to poke his brother, grab a toy, and then run off. What he did not account for was that his brother had grown a lot and was getting much stronger. Before Mark could escape, Brian reached out, powerfully grabbing a hand full of his shirt to stop his getaway. However, Mark had more muscle, being the older brother, and proceeded to start dragging his little brother clear across the house, with me following behind because I wanted to see this, of course! Mark lugged him all the way into the kitchen before Brian finally dragged him down and jumped on top of him to get back what Mark had taken, as they both laughed that deep belly roll kid laugh that anyone who is a parent or grandparent knows and loves!

Watching Brian interact with his brother in the hospital room, a new video reel formed in my mind of what may have happened there at the pearly gates when Mark was in his coma. I could see Mark trying to escape into heaven and Brian reaching out before he could get there, pulling him down while they laughed hysterically, with Brian screaming at his brother, "Oh no you don't sucker, I still need my brother here on this earth!" It made me laugh and appreciate how Brian had fought for his brother over those last few days and throughout their childhood together—in his red-headed Irish strong, silent, sassy way.

Next up in the room was my brother Chris. Mark smiled as he saw his uncle, though he could not remember him by name as such. Mark looked intently at Chris, recognizing but struggling to remember simultaneously, while my wife interjected, saying, "Mark, your uncle just wanted to come and say hello. Are you happy?" Mark nodded yes as he looked back and forth from Chris on one side of the bed to Hannah on the other. I knew it was hard for my brother to see him like this, yet it relieved him to see his nephew face-to-face and alive.

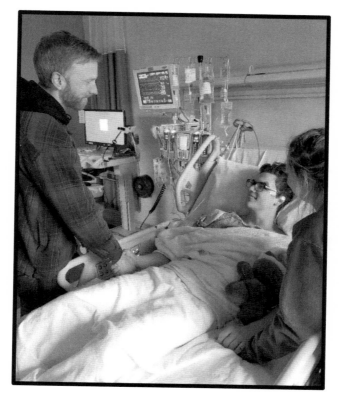

My brother Chris visiting with his nephew and
Hannah in the CCU Room on Thursday, 11/14

His next visitor would be his friend, Nikk Butler. Nikk had hardly left the hospital since Mark had gone in, so I knew it would mean a lot to him and Mark to see each other. Not to mention that Nikk is also a funny guy, so I knew he would make Mark laugh and did not disappoint while he was there in the room.

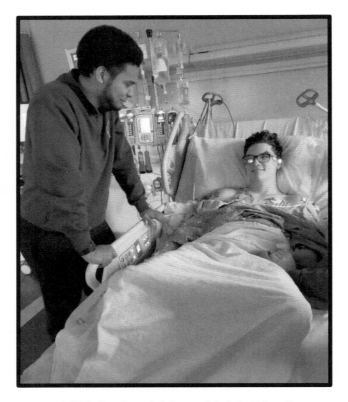

Nikk Butler visiting with his friend
in the CCU Room on Thursday, 11/14

With the significant milestone of that day out in the open, at last, we began to turn our attention to the next steps toward full recovery. After talking with the final visitor and taking the last photo for the day, I sat down at approximately 4:00 p.m. (that Thursday) to pen the next update to the warriors across the social media world, continuing to wait and pray for all of us.

Here is the big news we have been waiting for... Mark's MRI results showed only MILD damage to his brain from the head injury when he fell & the oxygen deprivation during the cardiac arrest!!!

Can you believe it?!! He just answered a number of questions from us and his doc and got 80% of them right. They stated that nothing his MRI showed should keep him from making a full recovery with time and rehab!!

He is eating applesauce, pudding, and ice chips now and off all the heavy machines they needed during the process. This young man is a living, breathable miracle!!

On the heart front... His original EKGs and X-rays days ago showed that parts of his heart were sluggish because of the trauma and cardiac arrests. Basically, if his heart was an 8-cylinder engine, only 6 of the cylinders were working. The latest shows that he is back to all 8 cylinders working in his heart!!!

Next steps... He will go in tomorrow afternoon for the coronary procedure to check all his major arteries as a precaution and prep for the Electrical Pulse (EP) Procedure that will be the last fix to wipe out those false electrical paths due to Wolff

Parkinson White syndrome. The EP procedure is currently looking like it will be on Monday.

I just don't have the words to describe what this picture represents... Sunday night, my son laid lifeless on the concrete for almost 15 minutes; his heart stopped with every sign that death was to be the only outcome.

Fast forward to today, and my son is back from the dead—smiling, laughing, talking, eating, recognizing almost everything and everyone already. He is literally the talk of this hospital as everyone is in disbelief but overjoyed to see how far he has come in such a short time!!

To all this, I say, JESUS is the way, the truth, and the LIFE! My life verse of John 14:6 has never meant more to me than it does right now. And to all of you, my brothers and sisters in this awesome family of God, I cannot thank you enough for your prayers and support. Please continue as he and we still have more to do, but God has provided miracles for every major obstacle to saving his life and beginning his full recovery! I love you all and thank you from the bottom of my heart!!

KEEP THE FAITH!!

Monument of Miracle

I had to re-read and re-write that post several times before I was able to send it as the fatigue was racking my body and brain harder than any point so far, in addition to the fact that I just kept finding more that I wanted to share.

I could not believe the difference that just 24 hours could make. I went back and read my update from 4:00 p.m. the day before. To have seen so much improvement since removing the breathing tube reminded me again that God was doing something special with my son. A story was being written before my eyes, the monument of a modern-day miracle.

CHAPTER VIII
ROUGH RIDE
TO WEEKEND WIDE

Whenever you see darkness, there is extraordinary opportunity for the light to burn brighter.

—Bono (Lead Singer of U2)

There had been so much to take in that day—along with relief came exhaustion, which fully enveloped my entire being as we moved into the late hours of Thursday evening. I had only had single-digit hours of solid sleep over the last five days and four nights, so I had physically, emotionally, and spiritually hit what felt like the great wall of China. I was 100% spent and physically hurting so badly. I knew it was time for me to get some rest and rejuvenate for what still lay ahead, though it was insanely hard for me to think about not being there with my son.

In truth, the push of being present I had put on myself was partially in hopes of taking my son's pain onto me. Every engaged father or mother understands this phenomenon that corresponds to a crisis. Thoughts of "what happens if you leave his side, and he takes a sudden turn for the worse?" plague the mind of every parent. This proved to be yet another area where I would have to trust God to watch over my son if I could go no further for the next short while.

Pulling Crystal aside in the CCU room, I asked if she was up to staying with him overnight, and she willingly granted me the reprieve. I went to Mark, who had been relatively calm throughout the evening, to tell him I was going home for a short while. As I did, I noticed how drowsy he also looked. The constant interruptions to whatever sleep his body was trying to acquire over the last 36 hours were stirring up a tornado within his body—he was also *fighting* sleep, because of his wide-awake nature, especially at night.

While Mark inherited the curse of insomnia from me, being unable to go to sleep is vastly different from constantly being forced to wake while you *are* sleeping. At times, he was visibly frustrated when they woke him to check on his blood sugar levels or the myriad of other care factors they were monitoring.

He still did not wholly comprehend everything that had happened to him, so I could understand why he was getting upset with what he saw as these weird strangers in smocks interrupting his slumber. I knew he hated to sleep, but it was more angering for him to subconsciously realize he needed it and not be able to get even one solid hour-long block of rest. He was managing to sleep off and on, but the combination of the drugs and intermittent waking was taking a toll.

As I finished telling my son I loved him and was going to get some much-needed rest, I also told him to try and get some sleep himself, but I knew that was not a likely outcome during the night as his mind and body continued to try and figure out what had happened. There were still questions to which Mark had no answers and ongoing gaps in his memory. Combine that nagging fact with a body wanting to rest but never being allowed to, and a nasty collision was on the horizon.

Rough Ride to Weekend Wide

The drive back to our house, shortly after 11 p.m., was much more peaceful than the previous ones, thanks to Mark's improvements, so much so that I recall fighting hard not to fall asleep all the way home during that 15-minute drive. I pulled into our garage, took a quick hot shower to wash all the hospital off, then fell into bed. I was out cold until my alarm went off at 6:30 a.m.

As I lay there in my bed, feeling insanely sluggish and trying to get my wits about me, I saw a text my wife had sent in the early hours of that Friday morning, November 15th, asking if I was awake. I knew that could not be good, so I quickly called her on the phone. What came back in her voice from the very first word broke my heart. Through another wave of motherly tears, she explained that Mark had suffered a setback.

As my wife tried to talk clearly through her crying, she shared the events that unfolded over about 6 hours throughout a rough night. As I had feared, the sleep deprivation and drugs had finally crossed paths with his pent-up frustration and lingering shock from the accident. Like a wounded lion coming face to face with unwelcome hyenas attempting to steal away what did not belong to them, the outcome within my son was volatile.

During those hours, Mark threatened an assisting male nurse with bodily harm to his man parts, cussed at his mom and his primary nurse (Madison), ripped out the IV, tried to remove other equipment cords from his body, and fought with anyone trying to help him. In truth, he was attempting to escape the room and how he felt—he wanted out of the *whole* situation!

Crystal told me that Madison tried to use her humor with Mark several times to get him to calm down and sleep, but she soon learned what we had known his whole life; when Mark sets his mind to something, there is no stopping that runaway train without appropriate measures.

Almost always, I have been able to de-escalate Mark, but without me there to try and do just that, they had no choice but to put Mark back in the arm restraints and back under the influence of heavy sedatives. Even with heavy sedatives, he warred against being back in the arm restraints because he could not comprehend what was happening to him. I knew that outburst had to be so hard for my wife to witness; it was a perfect example of what I'd been shielding both she and Hannah from since arriving at the hospital.

> **The contrast of calm countenance to seething struggle in a swift sliver of time is a sad shock to any observing soul.**

Crystal stated the worst part of the night for her came when Mark looked her in the face and whisper screamed, "Why are you doing this to me? Why won't you help me, Mom?" If her heart had been pulled from her chest and stabbed, it could not have been worse than seeing her son so desperately indignant!

As she finished telling me that Mark gave up the fight shortly before 6:30 a.m. and was finally sleeping soundly, I told her I was on my way, and we hung up the phone. I felt so terrible, guilty immediately, for her having to witness what she had with Mark. That was not her son—not her sweet, funny, caring boy that she knew so completely. Like the Hulk finally reaching his breaking point, Mark had snapped, not able to contain any longer the clash of physical and emotional conditions coursing through his entire being.

It was completely understandable and not entirely unexpected from a medical perspective, given all he had been through since coming out of the coma in such a short duration. Still, the contrast of his calm countenance merely hours before to the seething struggle that ensued during the midnight to 6 a.m. hours of Friday morning made it that much harder for my wife to watch the Dr. Jekyll to Mr. Hyde transformation of our son.

I gathered my backpack and everything we needed from the house and then returned to the hospital. When I arrived back in Mark's room shortly after 7:00 a.m., my wife fell into my arms and sobbed. After catching her breath, she explained that it made her so afraid to see him like that and to sense that his recovery had taken a staggering step back. She knew the facts, Madison had done a fantastic job, as usual, explaining that it was not uncommon for patients to react the way Mark did, but that data could not stop a mother's heart from hurting or worrying about what may come next.

We left the CCU room and went to the waiting room to eat some food and spend some time talking. Crystal was visibly exhausted and shaken by the turmoil she had just endured. I could see the apprehension in her deep blue eyes. Now there were new questions with Mark asleep again—questions we did not think we would have to contemplate since his coming out of the coma.

Would he wake up in a worse state? Did he indeed suffer a considerable setback in mind or body? Without saying a word, I knew these questions were there in her because they were there in me. Consistently over the next couple of hours, I reminded her verbally (as well as myself) of the progress he had made and that we needed to lean even *further* into faith—to *believe* that he was going to recover.

Around 10:30 a.m., the medical team converged on Mark's room for their daily assessment ritual. Upon hearing from the nursing team about all the struggles Mark had experienced through the night, they immediately decided to delay any other tests on Mark's heart until Saturday, depending on how the rest of the day and following night would play out.

I felt relieved, quite glad that there would not be any other major news on the state of his body happening this day. I wanted peace and rest for Mark and all of us as well. Watching him sleep in tranquility as we quietly talked with doctors was helpful. We held to the hope that this cessation of action on and around his body would pacify the traumatic frenzy that had pushed Mark over the edge the night before.

The remainder of Friday was uneventful—mercifully so. Mark slept hard, stirring only a few seconds several times throughout the day. This inactivity from him gave us all the chance to rotate in and out of the room, go outside for fresh air and sunshine, get food, talk about what had happened to this point, and supportively speculate on what may come next.

As the afternoon hours toiled on, I was amazed that Mark was still sleeping so hard. I kept saying aloud that his body needed it, so it was beneficial that he was not fighting sleep like he usually did. However, I am not sure I fully believed that. Likely, I was stating it that way to help myself cope, knowing that the enemy still lingered.

Death was back again, this time to peddle its latest liquid drug of fear—an elixir tasting of a lie that Mark got sucker-punched by his setback and was now spiraling downward toward the depths of darkness once again as he slept.

Each time that thought violated my mind—as death invited me to drink its drug—I pushed it away with the defiance which had already developed its firm stance within me. I would often close my eyes and say under my breath to death, "No, my son is alive, and I will not drink this liquor of lies. He is free from your clutches and on his way back to us." Yet, it was hard to open my eyes only to see Mark's eyes firmly closed and know he was slumbering in a place where no one could interact with him yet again.

> **Death will always reappear to peddle its liquid drug of fear, inviting us to drink and spiral downward to depths of darkness.**

Hours later, at around 7:00 p.m., my son finally woke. Instantly, something felt different. He took a deep, purposeful breath as he stirred, and I immediately felt a divine connection with that breath. It was unlike any he had taken since the start of this saga. It was the wind of change—a sign that his nearly thirteen-hour inertia had been an unconscious voyage back toward light and life rather than swallowing that nasty drug that death had tried to peddle to my soul earlier.

Looking into my son's eyes, I could see a glint of life that I had not seen since before his fateful falling. He was answering questions from the nursing staff and all of us faster and more confidently, though it was still very random, without a straight line, and absent typical rationale in his comments and responses. But I did not care in the slightest because of that glint in his eye—that gaze packed with hunger, like a grizzly bear waking from the cold, sleepy slumber of winter hibernation.

He was moving, eating, drinking, laughing, talking (softly), and interacting more consciously with everyone moving in and out of that room. It was fantastic! Mark was visibly gaining strength with each passing hour, and I teased him about the power of sleep, to which he laughed and said, "Yeah, yeah. When can I get out of here?"

Those words from his mouth matched the glint in his eye, revealing just a single word—resolve! I knew right then that my son was going to live on, and whatever challenges may still lay ahead with his rehabilitation, he was going to face it head-on, and we were going to be right there with him.

Nearly four hours after enjoying all the back and forth between my son and everyone who had visited with him, I retreated out to the waiting room a bit before 11:00 p.m. I needed to collect my thoughts, get another few deep breaths, and reflect on where we were—just five days removed from the worst day of my life. I felt exhausted for sure, yet exhilarated at the same time based on the miracle unfolding right in front of me.

As I sat on that uncomfortable couch, I had two thoughts. First, why in the world could the hospital not have offered more comfortable furniture to aid the bodies of those in crisis? I may have been more comfortable on a moss-covered log in the forest! Second, considering all that had happened to this point, I was overwhelmed with the unpredictable fragility and the undeniable resiliency of life.

I knew my last update to everyone connected to this story had been over 27 hours ago, yet it felt like only minutes had passed. I was anxious to share the next installment yet apprehensive that I would be unable to find the right words to explain the wonder of where we were in this progressing action drama. I remember thinking that I may want to write this whole story out one day. With that in mind, I knew that I could not overthink my next update or try to share too much information either. I picked up my phone, pressed the social media app button, and typed out my latest message.

Rough Ride to Weekend Wide

Ninth Post…
UPDATE on Friday, 11/15 at 11 PM (EST)

Mark had a very rough night on Thursday night as the trauma, drugs, lack of sleep, etc… really took a toll. He pulled out IV's and was combative, so he had to be put back in restraints.

That resulted in having to postpone the first cardiac procedure, which was supposed to be earlier today. But we knew this was going to be a process with ups and downs, and he is way beyond where we thought he would be just 2 days ago. So please pray for patience for Mark and all of us.

We want him back 100%, but that is going to take time and rehab. He finally was able to go to sleep around 6:20am this morning after that terrible night, and thank God he slept most of the day pretty soundly and woke up around 7pm in a much better state.

He stood up on his own for the first time and is now off all machines and the IV lines except the insulin to manage his T1D. Keep praying for his memories to come back and the process of that in the coming days/weeks because that cannot be rushed.

While the brain damage was mild, his brain is somewhat like a pinball machine right now... meaning that all the thoughts/ memories are in there, but he is bouncing randomly all over the place and has to relearn a straight stream of consciousness and timelines again.

Sometimes he remembers things well, then the next moment, he struggles. For example, he has called me Dad lots, but I have also been called Jimmy, Chaplain, and even Enrique.

How much of that has been Mark's humor mixed with sedatives and trauma, I don't know, but it is evident that it will take time, and there will be lots to re-learn and re-remember.

Pray for God's healing and complete restoration in this as well!!

Tomorrow morning we are scheduled for the first cardiac procedure to scope out his arteries. Then the EP study and the surgery to fix the WPW syndrome on his heart is scheduled for Monday.

Thank you all again so deeply for your relentless prayers and support for my son and our family!! The miracle of being able to sit next to him and have a conversation and laugh earlier tonight for a few hours was incredible! Love you all, and God bless you for your intercession on our behalf; we will never forget it!!

KEEP THE FAITH!!!

As I finished writing and re-read this post, I thought about the fact that it was Friday night. Usually, this was a night dedicated to celebrating the end of a work week by hanging out with friends and family at a restaurant or throwing a fun shindig at our house to laugh and enjoy life. I could not think of a bigger Friday night party to be at than the one I was present for on this November night of 2019. Instead of me having to send an update that my son had suffered a tragic accident and died, I was sending the next chapter of a miracle story God was writing during this wild week of our lives.

That night was a much more peaceful night of rest for us— we all seemed to exit Friday with a sense of serenity. I did not have to watch his every movement or listen to his every breath, wondering if it would be his last any longer. Those facts alone removed the levels of anxiety and grief that had been red lined in me since the previous Sunday, allowing me to close my eyes to sleep now that the flood waters of sorrow were starting to subside.

As the sun peeled away the dark layers of another night and awakened Saturday, November 16th, I felt eager to face the next foe of what was really happening with Mark's heart. The medical team came in mid-morning for their routine check-in and assessments.

After they finished, the first news they shared was that they had decided to postpone his first cardiac procedure to the morning of Monday, November 18th. I felt at the time like this was a poor strategy, mainly because there was something that still hid, an elusive enemy whom we did not remotely understand who was to blame for stopping his heart in the first place. The WPW within him felt like a sniper perched on a rooftop with a laser sight fixed on my son. Hence, I did not like waiting because I wanted to find this killer, run it to ground, and eliminate it—not give it more time to inflict damage on or in Mark's body but bring it to justice with a swift end.

Their reasons for postponing did make sense, as they wanted him to grow stronger for all impending procedures around his heart—to put a bit more runway between the trauma and when he would ultimately have surgery. I understood. On the other hand, it was difficult because I wanted my son to be entirely removed from danger and out of range of that sniper.

They explained that they would continue monitoring him thoroughly and could take abrupt action if his body gave any negative signs. That, combined with the fact that he had made such an incredible rise toward recovery over the last 48 hours, led me to concede that letting his body gain more strength before chasing down that sniper was the right strategy.

The cardiology team continued to express their amazement at his progress. They assured us that they would figure out what was going on with his heart—concluding that there were no serious threats to it based on the scans they had already completed. With all our questions answered, they left, with Monday as the new target to reconvene for the first of the additional heart tests.

Not long after that, the neurology team showed up again to reassess Mark, to elaborate on the results of his brain MRI and the road to recovery on that front. The chief neurologist on call (a different doctor than the previous chief) explained that while he was miraculously diagnosed with only "mild" brain damage, that still meant a long road of recovery ahead. As he started to fill in the blanks that they did not yet understand if all his motor skills would return fully, whether his speech would be in any way permanently affected, and that his memory may never entirely recover, I felt a jolt of unexpected shock.

He was sharing all this right in front of Mark, and as I looked at my son's face, I could tell he was trying to process all of it. I knew the doctor was trying to keep our expectations grounded, but I did not want that right then—I wanted unbridled optimism to form wings on Mark so he could fly into a full recovery that was not only possible but probable! I listened as he finished and purposefully avoided any other questions that would keep the conversation going so that he and his team would leave.

Once the room had emptied, Mark expressed that he was hungry, so I grabbed a chocolate pudding and started to feed him. However, I could feel skepticism toying with my mind and antagonism teasing my heart. This news that his "mild" brain damage could still mean changes to my son that did *not feel mild* had me rattled.

As I put the spoon into the pudding and then across the bed into my son's mouth, I was unconscious of what my face was speaking. I have always been good at hiding my natural transparency during a crisis to be courageous for those around me—but at that moment, the veil had cracked and what happened next was truly one of the greatest moments of my life.

I put the spoon back in the pudding cup, then turned my face toward the ceiling contemplating the uncertainty around my son. Suddenly, his raspy voice pierced my dissonance.

"Hey," he said to get my attention.

As I turned my head, surprised by the assertion in his voice which prickled in my ears, my eyes met his as I awaited his response.

"We got this!" he proclaimed with astounding assurance. I was rocked to the core by what I saw in his eyes and those simple words he articulated with acute perfection.

There was no doubt in his eyes, no distant far-off gaze that had been haunting me so over these last days. He was certain; he was convinced; he was confident. I was unaware that the veil had cracked in my countenance and revealed uncertainty on my face as I was feeding him, but my son saw it. He sensed that the neurologist's news had sparked skepticism in me, so much so that it moved him to respond to what he saw to reassure his father.

> **Surrender and resistance can exist within us simultaneously—as we surrender subserviently into the strong arms of life while we resist defiantly out of the dangerous clutches of death.**

In that flash, what I realized absolutely amazed me. God had joined with my son to speak *directly to me* at that moment— what I saw and heard from Mark's response was backed with the full authority of heaven and earth, making it undeniably apparent that God was present. It filled me with both surrender and resistance at the same time; surrender as I fell subserviently into the strong arms of life, resistance as I began to rip defiantly out of the dangerous clutches of death.

For those few brief seconds, I was speechless and overcome by the redemption of this reinforcement. I could not hold back my emotion or admiration as I put my hand on my son's head to respond.

"You know what, you are right, son, *we got this!*"

As I exclaimed those words to him, I felt that was the turning point I had been waiting for from Mark. It did not change the road that still lay ahead, but rather the inclination that this road was now leading to remarkable rescue instead of ravaging ruin.

The bedside interactions were different now; sounds of joy and laughter filled the room, and smiles flooded all the faces of those who sat next to my son.

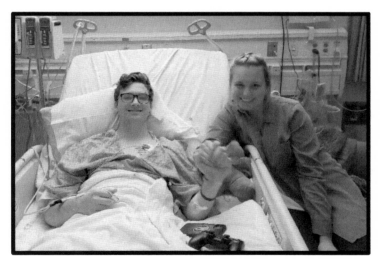

Mark and Hannah enjoying time
together as he recovers

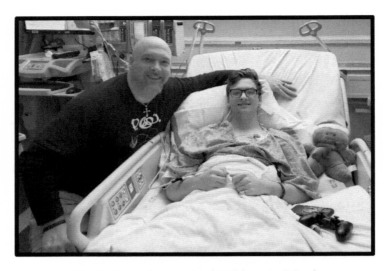

Kevin hanging out with his son Mark

We spent Saturday's remaining hours with visitors in and out of Mark's room throughout the afternoon and evening. It was incredible to watch the reactions of all the people as they visited with Mark, listened to bits and pieces of his story, and reveled in the relief of his still being alive. His memory was still erratic at best, but he remembered names, faces, and events of his life from before the trauma increasingly with each passing hour.

As he talked with his friends Sam and Connor, I asked him if he remembered the accident or anything since, to which he shook his head and answered, "No, I don't remember any of that." From Sunday night until he awoke on Friday evening— five days completely dark and missing from memory. It probably was for the best, given all that took place. Seeing him beam, talk, and interact with so many people again was an incredible sight and served as medicine to my soul.

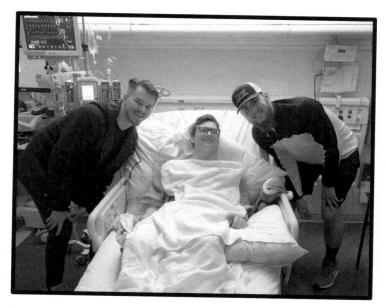

Connor Hash (left) and Sam Wilder (right) visiting Mark

One of the special moments came when Sam brought a gift of blue and red wristbands that he created for all of us, which had both Proverbs 30:30 (the verse from Mark's tattoo on his chest) and #Team Clayton printed on them. That meant a ton to us—a physical reminder that we could wear each day to continue to inspire us in helping Mark fully recover!

Thank you again, Sam, for your selfless acts in helping save my son's life physically, emotionally, and spiritually. Believe me when I say I will never forget it! You will forever hold a place of honor in the souls of my family and me.

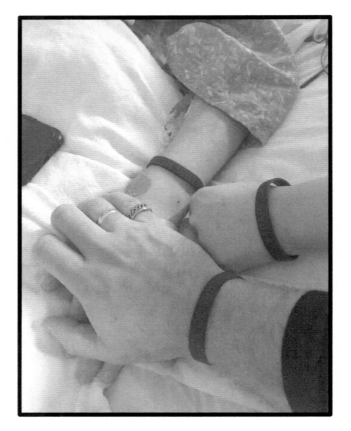

Father, Mother, and Son united
with the #Team Clayton wristband

As the day wound to a close, I was so depleted that I decided to forego the social media and email updates to the outside world. Honestly, I wanted to take in the news of this day for myself, reflect on the faces and reactions of visitors, and rest in my mind and spirit. It felt good to be free of the brutal fight against death and sorrow, so I wanted to give full attention to that self-status for a while.

Rough Ride to Weekend Wide

On Sunday morning, I woke with "we got this" still fresh in my mind. That reaction had left me dumbfounded the day before; now, I welcomed the determination that had exploded within me because of it. That was the Mark I knew, forever rebellious against being told that he cannot do something as I shared previously, so to observe that nature coming out of him again made me euphoric and filled my eyes with tears yet again. I know, there are a whole lot of tears in this story, but would it be any different if it happened to you?

Throughout the morning and early afternoon, amidst more visitors and doctor check-ins, there was a welcome sunniness that accompanied the Sunday spirit of rest and peace that was normal in our lives. It felt like a warm blanket after a long naked walk through frozen tundra.

The South Carolina sun seemed to shine brighter than the day before yet again, continuing to melt away the icy relics of our trudge through the frigid valley of death. Everyone who came in and out of that CCU room seemed to feel it and show it—a shining optimism derived from the progress we had all witnessed with Mark.

Later in the early evening, that optimism would culminate in the decision that Mark would be moved out of the CCU and into a regular hospital room! Can you believe it? In one distinct week, from Sunday to Sunday, my son transitioned from unresponsive on the brink of death to alive and well on the road to a viable recovery!

Even as believers in God before all this happened, we knew it was a week of rare miracles, but it becomes even more real when those apt to credit merely science or medical advances state in their own words that this young man is a miracle. The medical staff had started referring to Mark as "the miracle" in the days before, and it continued into Sunday.

He was disconnected from the machines that had held him in a state of "critical care" and then wheeled out of that CCU room ceremoniously to a standing ovation from all the CCU staff. They knew all too well with their inherent experience that it was uncommon for a patient who had suffered what Mark had to survive, much less be given a chance at full recovery! That said, the honor and gratefulness we felt in being able to transport our son out of the Critical Care Unit alive, not dead, cannot be overstated.

Being gifted such a profound miracle made us mindful and thankful for every person who contributed to getting us to the place of a happy exit from the CCU. On that note, I would be remiss if I did not share how I feel about two incredible medical professionals, in particular, Mike Gatlin and Madison Wilson.

The two of you shared the bulk of the nursing duty for my son, tagging each other in from day to night during our stay in the CCU. You each provided medical and personal care for Mark, which was stellar, thorough, compassionate, and selfless. I could not have endured such an insane trauma without either of you being there for my son, me, and my entire family!

Mike, your calm, steady demeanor and powerful positive attitude held me firm to the mission and the might it required. Thank you for the words you spoke in encouragement, the confidence and concern you carried on your face, and your courageous actions for my son—I am forever in your debt, and beyond blessed by the part you played in this miracle story!

Madison, your happy sweet character and nurturing, genuine spirit sustained me through the process we faced and the perseverance it demanded. Thank you for the words you spoke in reassurance, the strength and smile you carried on your face, and your brave actions for my son—I am forever in your debt and beyond blessed by the part you played in this miracle story!

Rough Ride to Weekend Wide

With Mark settling into his regular hospital room, it was time to update the outside world again. I made my way out to the general waiting room of the hospital, which was large and offered much more open space than the CCU waiting room (a welcome change of scenery), to pen out what was my tenth social media post and email.

Tenth Post...
UPDATE on Sunday, 11/17 at 7:30 PM (EST)

> *Mark continues to make remarkable strides in his recovery. He was moved out of CCU tonight to a regular hospital room!*

> *He was dubbed "the miracle" by all the staff in CCU. Mark's story has truly touched a ton of people, and it is so humbling to hear hospital staff talk about Mark as "the reason they do what they do." Truly it has been amazing to watch God work in so many ways.*

> *His first cardiac procedure is scheduled for tomorrow morning to check his arteries, and then Tuesday will be the procedure to fix the causes of the WPW syndrome.*

> *PLEASE PRAY that God will provide us positive results and no surprises on the results of both of those procedures!!*

Again, thank you, everyone, for your prayers to this point; you all are part of this incredible miracle story!!

THANK YOU, JESUS, FOR YOUR INCREDIBLE GRACE, POWER & LOVE!!

KEEP THE FAITH!

After posting my update, I sat back in the chair, took a maximum deep breath, then whispered a thank you to God above that the rough ride of Thursday night had led to a weekend wide with wonder. Now, we awaited in anticipation of getting to the heart of it all in the week to come.

CHAPTER IX
THE HEART OF IT ALL

*If through a broken heart God can bring His purposes to pass
in the world, then thank Him for breaking your heart.*

—Oswald Chambers

I had made it through what was undoubtedly the longest week of my life—which I am sure Crystal, Brian, Hannah, and everyone involved would wholeheartedly agree. It was only seven days, but it felt like months had packed themselves into those 168 hours filled with the extremes of an erratically swinging pendulum.

As I woke on Monday morning, November 18th, I heard the medical team's words from when Mark was coming out of his coma, "We'll try to have him out of the hospital by Christmas," ringing in my ears. It was poking at my brain as I remembered them saying it as a consolation that he was going to live but trying to set our expectations as well—in line with a long recovery based on the information they had at the time.

Moving my son out of the CCU the night before had signified that while typical recuperation periods were still being tossed forth by doctors, I reveled in the fact that God's rhetoric of recovery was contradictory with theirs in this story. It was already evident that Mark had blown away multiple dire prognoses by lying alive in his bed, rolling out of that CCU against all humanly calculated odds. That sentiment would thrust me into the week ahead as we faced ascertaining the actual condition of the heart beating inside my son's chest.

> **God's rhetoric of recovery is contradictory to the world's words of wellness.**

With each new morning, Mark awoke slightly more alert than the last. His memories were not yet restoring themselves entirely by any means, nor did he have the ability to be completely lucid all the time. It remained clear that the trauma had taken things that had not yet and still may not ever return to him. However, he was progressing in everything from motor skill tests to climbing out of bed to interacting more readily with all of us attending to him. Any degree of better for someone who had been dead just a week before is welcome and noticed straight away.

The time was upon us for the test series to analyze Mark's heart. The first was to investigate all major arteries. As they wheeled him out of his room this time, he was much more optimistic, as were we all. We comforted him that everything would be alright and affirmed how important it was to seek out all details of the actual condition of his heart. He grinned and looked relaxed as they disappeared out of sight and headed towards the Cath Lab.

Not too long after, or so it felt skewed by the ridiculous amounts of waiting on the razor's edge we had already undergone, they wheeled him back into his room. We gathered around and asked him how it went, to which he replied, "Good," quite casually. He could not grasp the tests' processes or importance. Just like that, it was back to the waiting game for the results once again.

Later in the early afternoon, the cardiology team arrived and delivered the message that he had passed the lab test with flying colors and all his major arteries were clear and undamaged! The chief cardiologist shook his head in amazement (yet again)—reaffirming that Mark was continuing to shock everyone with these results. However, he verbalized that he was still struggling to believe that such a catastrophic accident could have occurred only due to the WPW syndrome. Due to this reservation, he wanted to add a complete cardiac MRI to take an even more comprehensive look at his heart.

We knew he was not questioning the miracle at hand—as he himself had adopted to calling Mark "the miracle"—he wanted only to be thorough in his assessment which we appreciated immensely. He informed us the cardiac MRI procedure would happen the next day and then tentatively targeted Thursday, November 21st as the day for the ablation surgery, which was inevitable to fix the WPW. We thanked him again, expressing how thankful we were for the excellent care and attention to detail we were getting from him, as well as his entire staff, then he left.

I rotated in and out from the waiting room to Mark's room over the next couple of hours as the environment around his condition became more relaxed. My phone rang while I sat in his room, so I stepped out and answered the call. To my surprise, the person on the other end of the line was Brookley Cromer of Fox News (in South Carolina), who wanted to interview me about Mark's accident and survival.

Already feeling high from the great news of positive results after the first heart procedure earlier that day, this hit me like a lightning bolt and supercharged my entire body. Share my son's story?! Uh, yeah, duh! I pulled Crystal and Hannah aside in the hallway and gave them the fantastic news, then went to the waiting room to prep myself and pray about what I wanted to say.

A short while later, a few minutes before our agreed meeting time, I left the hospital, got in my truck, then drove into a commercial area across the highway where I would meet up with Brookley and her crew. We set up in a parking lot with the white, pink, and orange Prisma Health hospital directional signs behind her and a tree and vacant building behind me.

> **Stories are like stars; they burn hot and blindingly bright in the space closest to them yet shine a beautiful light from afar for others to gaze upon in wonder.**

My heart and mind were racing as her crew set up the camera and lights for the shoot. There was so much to tell! How was I going to cram this backdraft building inside me into the few minutes of a live interview?

I remember looking up, inhaling deeply, and then holding my breath for about 15 seconds as I looked up into the star-filled South Carolina sky. I exhaled gradually, fixing my eyes on the brightest star in the sky. It was a perfect representation sent from God above as to what would happen in this interview. This interview was just one among so many others throughout history telling of God's wonder. The bright star I chose to look at was only one of many in a sea of darkness above. Yet, I knew that this story served a purpose—to declare to anyone connected to my son, me, or my family the miracle God did for us right here in our present physical world.

Those stars seem so far off when we gaze upon them, but the reality is they burn hot and blindingly bright in the space closest to them—just as this story would burn hot and bright in the lives of everyone who knew it to this point. But it would not stop there; it would affect those who may come to know it both presently and in the future through word of mouth, a live news interview, or the pages of an eventual book. I knew I needed to relax and convey my son's story as succinctly as possible to this news outlet and let the outcome be what it may.

Life set the stage, the lights were hot, and the camera's red light switched on as I began to answer Brookley's questions and share the saga. Inside I felt like Aquaman trying to hold back enormous powerful ocean waves trying to break over me as I spoke. I focused on slowing my speech, speaking honestly from the heart, and most importantly, emphasizing the miracle Jesus did in bringing back my son from the dead.

I articulated the name of Jesus at least half a dozen times, God the other half a dozen times, and talked about the power of prayer. I wove through the pertinent details of my son's trauma; the two cardiac arrests, the oxygen deprivation, and his rare heart condition of WPW syndrome. Blurting out as much as possible while trying to hide my exhaustion and emotions as best I could, I gave my best effort to give glory to Jesus above for my son being alive and the miracle he was. The interview lasted 6 or 7 minutes, best as I can recall, then it was over.

After we finished, I thanked Brookley profusely for making the time and her willingness to bring this story to broadcast news. We exchanged information, and she shared the interview would go live on the 11 o'clock news later that evening. Her final request was for a short video of Mark recovering, which I knew I had from my brother, who took a great clip while talking to him in his room over the weekend. I thanked her again and then headed back to my truck.

As I climbed into the cab and slammed the door shut, I broke down. I sat in the quiet darkness behind my tinted windows, unable to hold back those waves trying to break over me any longer. Having just spoken publicly for the first time about our extraordinary ordeal over the last eight days, the telling of the story in interview style made aspects of it even more real to me.

My photographic memory flashed images through my mind—some that inflicted torment while others invoked unbridled elation. The magnitude of it all came hard like a tsunami, smashing my spirit once again with both the brazen reality of death as well as the blessed sanctity of life. Sitting there with my head pressed on the steering wheel, I sobbed, horrified by the incident, overjoyed by the aftermath, and unresolved by what near future secretly clenched in its hands just out of sight.

> **To simultaneously hate the tragedy,**
> **yet love the miracle, is the**
> **serendipitous force of story.**

As a man and father, those minutes alone in the cab of my truck were some of the most difficult and divided of my entire life. I honestly did not know what to think or how to feel—it was as if a surge of electricity from that interview had blown out all the circuit breakers within me.

The Heart of it All

I loved the miracle but hated the tragedy of this story all at once. Strange that such opposite forces can collide so violently in unison within human beings at times. How could I still feel sadness and grief while it occupied the same space as happiness and bliss? Is that possible? I did not know it at the time, but there was a gem hidden in all this riven disarray that I would come to understand later.

After about 10 minutes, I regained my composure and then spent the next five minutes or so breathing deeply again, as I had before, trying to inhale all faith and exhale all fear. I wiped off my face with napkins from the glove compartment, started my truck, then headed back over to the hospital to be with my family.

Arriving back in Mark's room, I excitedly relayed the details about the interview and told him it would be airing later that night. He joked about being famous after coming back from the dead and all, pointing out that few could say that in this life. I so love that my son has that humor to use as a weapon on command. However, even after he said it, he did not yet fully understand the second chance God was giving to him.

We picked up our dinner, shared some more time with Mark, and just before 10:00 p.m., I excused myself to the waiting room for the next update to the outside world. As I sat in the chair in a room only half-lit, snaps of the interview I had done with Fox News in the previous hours replayed in my head, but one sentence I had shared seemed stronger than all the rest right then. I had said, "We prayed hard the entire way to the hospital. I made a few phone calls to key people to start the prayer chain, and—*TRUST GOD*—there really is not a whole lot else you can do. At that point, to be perfectly honest, he was gone, so we just had to pray hard that God would do a miracle and bring him back to us."

The simple realization that God had indeed answered all those prayers spoken by thousands of people and achieved the miracle of bringing him back to us left me staggering and astounded. The civil war between mind and heart that I had felt right after the interview was suddenly a lopsided scale—one weighted overtly to the side of a heart exploding with nothing but thankfulness for the miracle of my son being alive! With that sentiment pounding from my heart, I penned out the next update.

Eleventh Post...
UPDATE on Monday, 11/18 at 10 PM (EST)

Mark completed the first cardiac procedure at the Cath lab today to check his major arteries and the results show no blockages, and his heart passages are totally clear!

The first major hurdle for his heart and God has come through once again with an answer to prayer!

They have added a cardiac MRI to the process to make sure he has no other issues in his heart. That is anticipated to happen tomorrow, and then the ablation surgery will likely happen Thursday as the final step.

Please continue to pray!! GOD IS AMAZING!!

Also, if you are here in South Carolina, they are running a story

The Heart of it All

about Mark on FOX News tonight at 11:00PM. Check it out if you can!

Thank you all for continuing to be part of this miracle in our lives!!

With another update dutifully delivered, I said a quick prayer to express my gratitude once more to God above and then made my way back to Mark's room to say goodnight. Crystal and I packed up all our stuff, hugged and kissed our son, and told him again how fortunate we were that he was alive. We told him we would record the news that night to save the interview and share it with him when he was ready.

With my wife's hand firmly gripped in mine, we stepped out of his room, rode the elevator down, ambled to our truck, and drove home. We talked about the events of the day, how happy we were at the progress Mark was making, and lastly, how amazing it was to be able to share this miracle story on the news.

Upon arriving home, I quickly set up the DVR to record the news while Crystal put a few things away, then we collapsed on our recliner sofa to wait for the story to air. It felt incredible to sit in those chairs—to rest together in the darkness, glancing over at each other occasionally, and completing each other's sentences because we were so drained that it was too hard to speak in entire sentences without help from one another. Then again, this is a pretty regular phenomenon for anyone married over 20 years.

We watched the news anxiously, talking during the ads, then finally the story came on. The aired story ended up being about 3 minutes long and well-constructed. Brookley effectively communicated his story, showed the video I had provided her of

Mark recovering, and finished by highlighting the GoFundMe that had been set up for him to help pay for medical expenses. It was a solidly reported and supportive piece for which I will always be grateful, so thank you, Brookley and Fox News; we appreciated the live coverage more than you know!

Once it finished and they cut to a different news piece, I looked over at Crystal, who was welling up again, and asked her what she thought. She said I had done a wonderful job with all I had said and that she was proud of me. That meant a great deal to me at that moment because she knew how tired I was and how harrowing this ordeal had been for me. I told her, "thank you," and kissed her hand. I stood up to stop the DVR recording and rewound it to watch it again.

Taking it in a second time, I was glad the piece included my son being referred to as a walking-breathing miracle, that it was all because of the power of prayer, and that "God" was named as central to the re-telling of the story. However, I noticed that every reference or phrase I spoke, which included the name of Jesus, had been edited out. The editing of my interview removed Jesus (specific) in favor of God (general) instead. I knew then and still know now that it was nothing personal, just standard reporting protocol in today's news world.

On the other hand, it served as sad evidence of the times in which we live—where the impersonal is preferred over the personal, political correctness is demanded over pure reporting, and theories of relativity are favored and far too often chosen over absolute truth. I was and still am disappointed to this day that censorship kept the name of Jesus out of my news; that the one who truly saved my son, the source of the real miracle, was left out!

It formed in me another dichotomy. There it was again, two feelings trapped inside me simultaneously—one supremely stoked that the story aired for the masses, the other undeniably upset that the unabridged story was left untold.

Let me ask you something. If someone had done a miracle and saved your child from the jaws of death, unequivocally without question, would you want the name of their rescuer unceremoniously removed from the story? No, you would not! No matter who you are or what you believe, if it happened to you, you would want that story relayed rightly without neglecting your beliefs or omitting eyewitness perspectives.

My wife and I talked about it for a few moments, mainly because I wanted her to know that I had shared so much more directly and purposefully about Jesus (specifically) as the one who showed up in power and brought our son back from the dead. We also discussed that the omission revealed a cultural cavity we are experiencing currently in our country—true freedom of speech and freedom of religion are understood and agreed with in *theory*, yet not unconditionally embraced and practiced in *reality*.

The news far too often does not capture or relay the whole story as it was experienced by those living it or telling it. However, before I stray too far off point, those are subjects for another time, another place, a different book. My reason for sharing my position on those things here is that something settled in my soul right then and there in my living room; I would need to tell this uncut story—a miracle through a father's eyes—so that all may know it *in its entirety*!

While I felt frustrated that (from my perspective) a key person had been left out of the news, Crystal and I mutually agreed that the miraculous, the power of prayer, and God were all included, which came through forcefully. So, we released our frustration and prayed that the story would impact someone, somehow, both that night and in the future.

Tired and ready for a good night's sleep, we powered down all the electronic equipment, showered off all the hospital again, and dropped into bed. We even both took melatonin to make sure we got our rest, which turned out to be a great decision.

When the sun broke into our bedroom on Tuesday morning, November 19th, we both felt renewed yet distinctively eager to return to the hospital. I remember saying to Crystal as we were getting ready, "I can't wait to see what God is going to do today with our son."

Both of us shared clear anticipation that this rise we had seen over these last days would continue today—we *believed* it as it resonated from our voices and emanated from our spirits.

We arrived back in Mark's room a little after 8:00 a.m. and were happy to hear that Mark got a bit of decent rest the night before and he seemed a bit more perked up than the day before. We shared the news interview from the night before with him via my smartphone as I had recorded it as they were airing it live, and he loved the piece. His smile, blue eyes, and overall body language exuded a healing essence and greater tenacity now, which we ate up like hogs at a local buffet.

Later the cardiology team showed up for their daily evaluation of his condition. Not long after that, pleased with his continuing improvements, they wheeled him out of the room again to undergo the clinical cardiac MRI. He threw up his thumb and smirked big as he headed out of sight, making us laugh.

I turned to Crystal and said, "Hakuna Matata!" She giggled loudly and stared me down with her big blues, which made my heart bulge to see her smile and laugh there in that hospital corridor.

The Heart of it All

Short tests we appreciate. Short waits for test *results* are appreciated even more, but the cardiac MRI procedure on this day took time. Honestly, I cannot remember exactly how long it took, but it felt much longer than the Cath Lab procedure from the day before. That always makes your mind run—did they find something that concerned them? Did they run into complications? Each time one of those pessimistic pests of paranoia crept into my psyche, I pushed it out! I just refused to entertain them any longer in favor of bold belief.

> **Never allow the pessimistic pest of paranoia to creep into your psyche and position a permanent presence.**

When they finally brought Mark back, he seemed tired and irritated. He confessed that he was getting sick of all the tests, the check-ins, and the less than impressive hospital food. He wanted to go home.

We agreed with him, affirming we felt the same way and that if we successfully cleared these test results, the only thing left was the ablation surgery itself. That was music to his ears as he joked again, "Y'all gotta get me outta here before the bad food and uncomfortable bed kill me! I didn't come back from the dead for all that. I want a fat bacon burger and my big bed," he threw out in his funny-man voice, which was now almost back to full strength.

We now spent the time between procedures and results with games, TV, and conversations to fill the space and keep his spirits up as best we could. That is hard to do with a driven personality like Mark—he had stated his desire to go home, and if left up to him, he would have disrobed and walked up out of that joint instantly!

Early evening rolled around, right before the dinner hour, and the chief cardiologist made his way to Mark's room. He did not beat around the bush this time, quickly stating that Mark passed the cardiac MRI perfectly. He said he surprisingly saw nothing of major concern and was ready to perform the surgery the next day as the decisive step in addressing his heart!

I seriously wanted to break dance on the floor or go full "Gangnam Style" (Google it) when that preposterous news hit my ears. With God giving him wings, this kid of mine was thrashing every obstruction standing in his way and silencing every naysaying critic.

Jacked out of my ever-loving mind with my adrenaline gland wide open, I probably could have lifted my truck off the ground and tossed it aside if I had been out in the parking lot at that moment. The warrior in me knew that we definitely had the location of that sniper inside my son now. Tomorrow the surgeon would hunt it down for good at long last!

Reaching the place where all the tests were behind us had me flying inside. I knew we still had surgery in front of us. Still, it seemed as if I had the eyes of an eagle now, better able to see all that was happening, viewing the larger landscape of the vicious valley we were walking out of in favor of a brightly lit path up to a miracle mountaintop.

After getting food in my belly and sharing good laughs around the dinner table in the hospital cafeteria area, I pulled out my phone at around 7:00 p.m. and penned out the next update to the outside world.

The Heart of it All

Yet another answer to prayer from God today as the Cardiac MRI came back totally clear!! I am so amazed and humbled by God's ongoing protection and healing for my son.

Only one more major hurdle to go... Tomorrow afternoon (tentatively scheduled for 3pm Est), he will have his ablation surgery in which they will eliminate the false electrical paths that caused the cardiac arrests. PLEASE PRAY for this final step and the doctors performing the procedure; that it will be a complete success!

Again, thanks so much to everyone for sticking with us in this prayer war and on this miracle journey.

God is faithful...

KEEP THE FAITH!!!

That post felt so redeeming, so full of life. I could sense the crowd of eyes watching and the countless hearts fully invested in this saga—I could hear all the people's prayers that had carried us through.

Awe had taken hold of me because of what God was writing in this chapter of our lives. I knew it was continuing to spread, and I stood excited that the boundaries of this story would expand even further. Now, finally, we knew the heart of it all and stood ready for a surgery and storybook finale.

CHAPTER X
SURGERY & STORYBOOK

When our willingness collides with God's power,
an inconceivable unfolding of purpose erupts.

—Tim Tebow

As I lay in our bed after returning home from the hospital on Tuesday night, I struggled to get to sleep. Insomnia is unpredictable at best, and its reasons are quite cryptic or complex most times, but tonight the reason presented itself quickly.

The cardiologist had not given us a time frame for when Mark might be released from the hospital as it would be based solely on the outcome of the surgery the following day. This fact brought to bear the burden of possibilities of his "going under the knife," so to speak. I had never heard of ablation surgery before, so I grabbed my smartphone and looked it up to research for myself.

The data I discovered was that it usually was merely an outpatient procedure that took, on average, about 75 minutes, was commonly practiced with a high percentage of success, and encountered few adverse reactions or side effects. This information brought me a certain amount of peace inside. Enough peace that after a few minutes of heartfelt prayer for

God to finish this miracle with a successful surgery on my son the next day, I was able to kill those pessimistic pests of paranoia that had reappeared once again and fall asleep.

I slept for a solid seven hours that night, despite having interesting dreams and, according to my wife, having a few flinches, which obviously meant I was fighting something or someone as I slept. Those flinches were a foreshadowing of how I felt when I woke up. I was ready for a fight!

Bring on this surgery, bring on that sniper still hiding inside my son, bring on evil, bring on death, bring it all on. I was fully engaged in defiant faith, ignoring consciously every negative "what-if" in favor of the facts of every small battle we had won over the last week since he had come out of his coma—choosing to believe now that we would indeed *win this whole war*!

Rolling over to gently wake my wife, who was also stirring, I whispered in her ear, "Today is the grand finale to this crazy miracle, my love. Our son is alive, and I believe with my entire being that God is going to finish what he started in bringing our son all the way back to us!"

She turned over, looked into my eyes, and said, "Are you sure? I want that so bad. I just want my son's heart to be all right."

I responded emphatically, "I am ridiculously sure! Just think about what Jesus has done since our son woke up. He did not bring us all this way without purpose. Mark is a miracle, and while I know he still has memory to recover, motor skills to regain, and muscle to reclaim, I also know whatever happens today in that surgery, we *will* reach a positive end."

We laid there in bed for a few minutes and held each other, breathing in deep, then praying together before getting ready and leaving the house to head to the hospital.

I felt a different presence walking through the hospital doors this time—the presence of light, love, and life. There were still unknowns about the surgery that would come later that day, but I felt in my soul a safe trust for God as well as the surgical team that would operate on my son.

> **Always keep your head mindful and your heart redolent to what the simple things in life really mean.**

Arriving in Mark's room, we immediately saw that he again looked better than the day before. He was a bit more alert, more physically active with his gestures and movements, and his voice more potent. That provided an immediate visual affirmation in my heart to what I had felt waking up earlier that morning—he was rising back toward life in its fullest form!

Sitting down next to my son, I talked with him about this being the day we would get into his heart to repair it. I intentionally tried to keep the mood light by saying, "That's nothing new though, son, right? God and I have been poking around inside your heart your entire life, so this time we'll let the doc have some fun in there for a little while!"

That brought forth another big grin with laughter, and he quipped back, "He'll probably find some Star Wars and Marvel stuff in there." This comment stems from the fact that he is a huge nerd; oops, I mean, he is a massive fan. So am I, truth be told, so nerd up with all the light sabers, blasters, shields, lightning hammers, red tech suits, and giant green monsters you can muster y'all!

It brought me such hearty happiness just to be joking around with my son. I was not able to do that just one week earlier, so again, my head was mindful and my heart redolent of how much this simple, playful banter really meant to me. The nightmare of having to live without it had been banished for the time being.

The cardiology team arrived a bit before noon and talked us through the process of the ablation surgery. In short, the procedure is finding the extra sensory path growing on the outside of the heart and then literally burning it off so that false electrical signals can no longer confuse it. This process reverts the beating muscle to the correct method of sending signals from top to bottom through the biological regulator present in the human heart.

As I stated previously, the typical duration for the outpatient surgery when they catch WPW syndrome early is only 60 to 75 minutes. However, his surgeon quickly conveyed that the process and time involved for Mark would be different.

He was honest and told us that despite all the positive heart scans and tests, the sheer statistics of how rare it is to have such catastrophic circumstances around only WPW still had him convinced that there might be another issue with my son's heart. That said, the only way for him to be sure there *were* no other issues would require him physically cruising around inside Mark's chest during the surgery. He told us the surgery time would likely be double the standard duration, about two and a half hours, possibly even three in total.

Additionally, he assured us he was not stating there *was* something else wrong, but merely that he had to be sure there was *not* by spending the time necessary to cover every square inch of Mark's heart. My mind immediately dashed to that sniper—imagining that ghostly figure trying to sneak back into the shadows as we hunted it down. I remember saying to the surgeon, "You take all the time you need because we want to be sure no other dangers are lurking in his heart!"

Lastly, he told us that surgery prep would begin around 3:00 p.m., with the surgery start time landing at approximately 4:30 p.m. if all went according to plan. The time for the final battle was set. I looked at my watch, and while I did not remember the time, even though I knew it went into my head, it was more the realization that we were mere hours now from facing and eliminating the rarity that started this whole death and back journey. I felt ready.

> **A constant stream of trusting thoughts, willful words, and provoking pleas lifted to heaven is the invitation for a miracle in everything we encounter.**

I do not remember much about the hours between finding out when the surgery would be and when they arrived back in the room to start the transfer process. Looking back now, I was hyper-focused on praying. These were not prayers with my head bowed and eyes closed. No, it was a constant stream of trusting thoughts, willful words, and provoking pleas lifted to heaven as I multi-tasked talking and listening to my son and others.

If only one could have seen inside me during those hours. I was a man standing waist deep in a burial hole in the middle of a graveyard with arms fully stretched to the right and left of my body, head tilted back to gaze above, and eyes wide open. Streams of energy, positivity, light, hope, and unsullied petition rose out of my soul like a gushing reverse waterfall. There amidst angels lifting a being out of a grave in the ground, I would have let my very life be withdrawn from the whole of my body and soul to give my son his life back fully.

Like a loud crack following a silence, I was jarred from my meditative state as it was wheels up while we followed Mark as they transported him into the cardiology wing of the hospital a little after 3:00 p.m. They informed us that the prep room was not large, so only Hannah and I went back to be with him during the process leading up to surgery.

The room would vacillate for the next 90 minutes from abuzz to hushed. Hannah and I talked off and on with Mark and each other. The times in between the conversation allowed me to return to my meditative state.

As we passed the official start time of 4:30 p.m., I grew charged to start the chase for that sniper within my son, and every minute after was tense for me. I occasionally clenched my fists in my lap. I inhaled intensely, symbolic of the swelling desire I felt within to begin this last battle so that the entire war may finally reach its epic conclusion.

No sooner had I finished another deliberate inhale than the trumpet sounded that the battle was to begin as the nurse entered the room and blurted out, "It's time!"

Hannah and I spoke our final words of encouragement and confidence to Mark, then we each physically touched him once more to connect with him. They whisked my son in one direction toward the operating room while Hannah and I went opposite, back toward the cardiology waiting room.

It felt so different to walk away from him this time. There was still the extant reality that anything could happen during surgery, yet more overpowering in me was the ardent actuality of the restoration over the last week—he was alive and becoming more so every day! That actuality is where I chose to harbor my heart and secure my soul as I said one more whispered prayer in that hallway as Mark headed for where he would go under the knife.

Back in the waiting room, yes, waiting again, we settled into different hospital-type chairs. We were restless, to say the least, repeatedly re-positioning as the minutes went by. Nikk and Justin returned to the waiting room to be with us, which led to prayer and then laughter after that, which helped us all pass the time. Hearing Brian laugh and tell stories about Mark with those two knuckleheads (you know I love you guys) was therapeutic for Crystal and me.

On the waiting room wall was the "Status Board" TV monitor, which provided the various phases of the surgery process and active patient updates. The first hour and fifteen minutes seemed to pass faster than I had anticipated, thanks in no small part to the entertainment of the young bucks hanging out with us.

However, once we got past that allotment for a standard outpatient ablation procedure, time turned into that stupid slinky hourglass again, seemingly sifting every grain of sand through that skinny center passageway in slow motion. Every five minutes, I would stare at the monitor on the wall, begging my eyes to find a status other than "In Surgery," staring back at me like a tiger hiding behind a dark thicket in the jungle.

Passing beyond two hours, the words of the doctor began to play like a broken record in my head when he had said, "Best case, I am done in 90 minutes, but if I find something else, it could push the surgery time up to two or even three hours. I just won't know until I am there inside Mark's heart."

All I could do was pray and keep resetting my wandering mind back to the restoration from Wednesday *then* to Wednesday *now*. Nonetheless, it grew harder and harder to incarcerate the imagination of what was happening inside my son's heart back in that operating room as every 60 seconds elapsed.

Shortly after 7:15 p.m., it happened. BOOM! I glanced up at the monitor, and his status changed to "Post-Surgery." His operation had reached its end! The fact that the doctor had not come to retrieve us during the process meant that nothing life-threatening had taken place, which was the immediate relief we all felt in our hearts.

Only a few minutes passed, and his cardiologist came out to provide his surgical summary. First, he explained that he went up through Mark's femoral artery with a scope and tools. Second, he sped up his heart which led to the discovery of the extra pathway on the outer wall of his heart. However, the increased heart rate triggered a false signal from that extra pathway which led to another cardiac arrest. He quickly comforted us with that being an expected reaction of the body during this procedure which required another defibrillation to put the heart back in a regular rhythm. Third, as mentioned earlier, he burned off the abnormal pathway, completing the ablation. Lastly, he sped up his heart again to look for any issues related to WPW syndrome or other cardiac functions.

As he promised, the surgery ended up being about two hours and twenty minutes, give or take, as he explored every millimeter of Mark's heart. He was looking for anything else, any other hidden snipers that may try to inflict damage on my son in the future.

He shook his head slowly as he was arriving at the climax of conclusion and said, "I thought for sure I would find something else wrong with his heart because he is so young to have such a catastrophic accident, but I'll be danged, the only thing wrong with Mark's heart was that WPW which we fixed. Mark is going to make a full recovery!"

I responded quickly, saying, "That son of mine really is a miracle!"

He quipped, "Yes, yes, he is! I am so happy for all of you that he is alive, and we were able to fix his heart."

As this was not a routine outpatient surgery because of circumstances leading up to it, he decided to keep Mark in the hospital overnight as a final precaution. He then relayed the unbelievable news that unless there were any unexpected complications (which he did not anticipate), they would discharge him to go home the next day. Those welcome words quenched like a glass of cool water after being in the driest desert for ten straight days!

We all thanked him with as much fanatic gratitude as we could muster in our mixed state of exhaustion and elation, then I immediately fell into my wife's arms while we both shed more tears of joy and relief. I looked into her eyes and said, "Mark is healed. Our son's heart is going to keep on beating. He is a living, breathing miracle, resurrected from the dead!"

The only words she could utter in her emotion were, "I am so glad my son is alive. I love my Markie!"

There was a celebratory riot rocking in my heart like none I had ever felt before. Imagine the sound of all the people in the whole world exploding into applause, screaming, whistling, and dancing simultaneously—that was the scene happening within me. It was obnoxiously yet wonderfully rowdy, and I knew I had to share this with the world outside who were waiting on the latest word.

Lifting my smartphone, I penned out the news, knowing it would fail to fully relay the exultant sentiments I wished to convey at that moment, though I would give it my best effort anyway.

Thirteenth Post…
UPDATE on Wednesday, 11/20 at 7:30 PM (EST)

> *Mark just came out of the final surgery, and I am stoked to tell everyone that they found and fixed the problems with the extra path on his heart, and he should be able to go home tomorrow!!!*
>
> *God is so big, so faithful. He saved my son's life and has granted him positive results at every major hurdle!!*
>
> *He and we are all exhausted, overjoyed, and grateful beyond belief to Jesus for his power and healing!! But ready to go home and start the next chapter of all our lives…*
>
> *We also are beyond thankful to all of you who have followed this miracle journey and prayed relentlessly with*

us for Mark's life, surgeries, and full recovery!!

He will need to rest for a while, and it will take time for all the neurological pieces to come back together, but Mark survived, and I can't wait to see what God holds for his future!!

THANK YOU!! KEEP THE FAITH FOREVER!!

Hitting the send button on that post and email update was and will forever remain one of the most extraordinary snapshots of my life. To this day, when I read it, I am but a time traveler dropped right back into that raucous riot of celebration, screaming so viscerally that my voice is vacated.

> **Let the revelation of things overcome sink deeper and grip your soul for as long as you live!**

Closing my eyes there in the waiting room, I dropped my head in a vain attempt to absorb the roar of this fully realized redemption, shaking my head at the sovereignty of a God who holds power over death itself.

Mark was going to be in post-Op for at least an hour. Knowing I had time before they would transport him back to his hospital room, I decided to make a food run because I was starving after going for hours with nothing more than nervousness for my stomach acid to try and digest.

I also knew I wanted to absorb a few meditative moments alone in my truck to allow the revelation of all we had overcome in these last days to sink deeper and truly grip my soul. Closing my eyes again, I scrolled through the pages of my mind, one by one, consciously viewing both the risk and outcome of every procedure that Mark had endured each day since waking from his coma.

It was astonishing to relive each event and its corresponding positive result. God did not owe that to me or any of us—it did not have to turn out this way. There were so many things that could have gone wrong but instead went right. So many tragedies that threatened, yet they were all turned away triumphantly!

Opening my eyes, my face teeming with tears, I turned my head again to heaven above and literally screamed aloud, "Thank You, God, for saving and healing my son! I know you didn't have to, but I am so grateful he is still alive and with us here on this earth!"

Doesn't it feel so good to scream sometimes? To purge all the pent-up fury, give up the grotesque grief, and release all the recoiled rage from the deepest wells of your emotions. Oh, if you happened to be walking by my truck as I was screaming that day, sorry, I did not mean to scare you, but under the circumstances, I am betting you can understand.

Feeling altogether alive again, at last, I reached over to my stereo, cued up the song "Alive" by P.O.D., and drove down the road rocking as my ears burned to heavy guitars and drums. At the same time, I sang at the top of my lungs with Sonny the uplifting words of what it means to *feel* alive and *be* alive!

Returning to the hospital, it felt righteous to eat tasty food, have enjoyable conversations, and know that tomorrow was shaping up to be great with going home as a tangible reality instead of a distant delusion.

With Mark fully conscious and settled in well for the night, we returned home to what we confidently claimed was the last night we would have to sleep with our son in the hospital.

I cannot remember if the sun was shining the next morning or not. With it being South Carolina, it most likely was, but it did not matter because the sun in all its shining splendor was radiating from the inside out. Arriving back at the hospital, I was so excited, ready to escort my son out of that valley and back into the panorama of his life ahead.

The day seemed to drag, primarily because of all the discharge processes involved in getting out of medical prison. After much ado about the last questions, paperwork, and gathering up all his things as we waited, it was finally time. He was standing, got dressed in the bathroom, then sat down in the wheelchair to be wheeled out. It was a surreal scene for all of us as we exited that room.

To be walking next to Mark, alive and well, with him cracking jokes about finally being out of that lousy bed, wanting to pound real food for days, and having a second birthday after returning from the dead—it felt incredibly spiritual and lauded by the realms of heaven!

We rolled him out of the front doors, helped him into Hannah's car, and followed behind them as they drove back to their apartment. Upon pulling up, Julie (Hannah's mom) was waiting in the parking lot with Kovu. When Mark got out of the car, needless to say, he got attacked by a dog who had missed his daddy terribly. It was such a grand sight to hear Mark react and Kovu bark while he embraced and wrestled his black shaggy buddy as they enjoyed being back together finally!

Mark reunited with his dog, Kovu,
on Thursday, November 21st, 2019

After his fabulous reunion with man's best friend, we helped Mark get into his apartment, loaded in all his stuff, then left him to begin the recovery process at home.

When we pulled into the garage at our house, we left all our stuff in the truck, went inside, and ultimately collapsed. After an hour of talking and resting with my wife on the recliners in our family room, I picked up my smartphone to close this saga with one last update to the outside world.

Fourteenth & Final Post...
UPDATE on Thursday, 11/21 at 4 PM (EST)

> *Mark was discharged from the hospital today and is now home!! His dog Kovu freaked out and was ecstatic to see him!!*
>
> *Thank you all, who supported us selflessly and prayed so vigilantly for Mark as we were living out this miracle journey over the last 11 days.*
>
> *May it forever be a reminder to us all that Jesus is King, a king who conquered death and brings life, who pours out unconditional love, and blesses us with healing, even to the point of turning back death itself!!!*
>
> *Mark Clayton, my son, you are a survivor with a lion's heart, and your fighting spirit is an inspiration; I am*

honored to be your Father in this life!!

Writing those concluding words that held such vast victory was incomprehensible and entrancing. I hit send, and just like that, it was over; the whole ordeal was finished. All the trauma, all the tests, all the procedures, and heart surgery were done. All the waiting, worrying, and wondering—beautifully resolved in perfect accord.

Mark made it through, unbelievably, miraculously, with each positive outcome outshining its pessimistic oppressor. His heart was healed, his mind was mending, his future was full, and his soul was safe. My son had been spared—though death had come calling him by name, life would rise to reveal a miracle that this father viewed through his own eyes.

Sitting there in a near paralytic state, the gravity of it all met the levity of it all, creating a new canvas colored with dark death on one side and light life on the other. I had seen this picture before, so I thought, in stark contrast, with death and life each undeniably separate, never touching at all.

However, in looking closer, there were no longer two distinct sides but rather colors that bled artistically across the center line as if they expressly belonged one to another. Death and life, painted individually yet intrinsically in perfect unity, for all to imagine and behold.

CHAPTER XI
NO DEATH, NO LIFE

There is no easy walk to freedom anywhere,
and many of us will have to pass through the valley of the
shadow of death again and again before we reach the
mountaintop of our desires.

—Nelson Mandela

Where the path of life passes into the pitch black of a long cave where death inflicts itself without remorse, an invisible truth shrouds itself within. It is not a truth one can reach just by standing at the edge gazing in; no, it requires fully immersing yourself in the cave. It cannot be extracted from the side, above, or below—you must travel every step to the rear of this cave before the truth reveals its incognito. This prerequisite means that before we can unearth the enigma there at the end, we must traverse death in all its varied duplicitous forms.

As I stated in my introduction, death is not limited only to the *physical* realm; it preys upon our thoughts, emotions, and souls. Most of us have already faced its most prevalent form in the expiration of a human being connected to our own life—a grandparent, parent, child, friend, or colleague who passed on. Yet, rarely do we acknowledge the other forms of death that are much more sinisterly active in our *daily* lives.

Death is a darkness that blackens every beam of light as it hollows the heart, melts the mind, and starves the soul. Death is the ever-present evil that elegantly entraps emotions.

Death is the sickening selfishness that slowly suffocates our spirit. Death is the fear which feeds on faith, forgiveness, and fidelity. Death is the cruelty that creates captivity and crushes compassion.

Death is the betrayer of belief, the cheat of contentment, the killer of kindness, the murderer of meaning, the assassin of aspirations, the destroyer of dreams, the executioner of encouragement, and the slayer of satisfaction.

Yes, death is also the calculating cancer that coldly corrupts every living cell, the deadly disease that devastates our divine design, and the vicious virus that violates our verity. I think it is safe to say that no one wants to face tumors, cancers, viruses, or diseases, which all have the capability to end our physical existence in this life.

Pain associated with the physical form of death is acute; it ruins our bodies, imbrues our emotions, and assaults our souls whether we ourselves are dying or someone else in our life is dying. There is a finality to it; hence, we recognize it readily, run from it relentlessly, and try to hide from its hollow subjugation.

However, should this be our response to *any* form that death would take in our lives?

Because it is so powerful and life-altering in its carnal form, we understandably can end up projecting that singular comprehension onto *all* forms in which death would disguise itself. We know the bodily form of death well; it is obtrusive and announces itself boldly without a shred of secrecy. Yet I believe it does so in this form to hide its other more sneaky, subtle, seductive figures.

Are you ready to shake hands with death?

— William Tiptaft

You have heard me state this already, death is inevitable—how we feel about it, whatever our experience has been with it, we cannot escape it. That said, our *complete* understanding of death is critically important if we are to deal with its inexorable interruption in our lives.

William Tiptaft, a 19th Century preacher, once asked, "Are you ready to shake hands with death?"

At first, that sounds morbid, overtly ominous, don't you think? Who in their right mind would want to shake hands with death? Willingly reach out and embrace the icy fingers of the grim reaper? Nobody, if our understanding of death begins and ends with the horrifying images and realities of agony, tears, loss, or absence.

Let me be crystal clear on one crucial point before any more words are written—shaking hands with death does *NOT* mean contemplating, or God forbid, committing suicide!

Suicide is the sharpest and sickest tool ever wielded by the devil himself. He uses it to rob someone of their physical existence so they can never experience life after death here on earth as God intended. There is no greater tragedy than a poor soul so burdened that it would give in to ending their own life! You, the reader of these pages, have infinite value to God and the people in your life. Do not forsake, ever, the truth that *your life matters*!

Ok, now we can continue.

Shaking hands with death does not mean you have to admire it, desire it, allow it to take more than it should when it appears, or invite it to stay as a permanent resident in your psyche or soul.

Shaking hands with death simply means acknowledging that it is *one* shady character in the complete story of life as we know it. Recognize that it will visit you again and again throughout your life—*accept* that it will take something from you each time it comes.

Death never leaves empty-handed; its purpose is to rot what is right, poison what is pure, decompose what is dignified, and steal what is sacred. Corroding all it touches, its only craving is to slyly slip away with strength, joy, peace, hope, and even love itself.

Think about it. You are successfully working a job you have been in for years when you are suddenly laid off or forced to resign without cause or notice. That is a form of death—it came to steal your security, leaving insecurity instead; it robbed resources required by you and your family; it pilfered the peace and prosperity of your current plan as well as your planned future.

Death does not apologize either. It is faceless, offers no solutions, and chillingly does not care even in the slightest.

Think about it another way. You meet an exciting person that quickly turns into what you feel is a unique "true" friend. For years you talk for hours on the phone, hang out at each other's homes, take vacation trips, and share incredible memories (both good and bad) as you walk through life with one another. Then, abruptly they change and disappear from your life either with or without explanation. That is a different form of death—it came to fleece your faith in friendship, trash your instincts of truth and trust, and ruin what ought to be one of the most real relationships.

Death does not empathize either. It is nameless, offers no answers, and callously does not feel even the least little bit.

Think about it one last time; a bit different still. You get married, blissful and happy from the very beginning, waiting animatedly to see your new spouse each day. For those first few years, you laugh big with (and at) each other, enjoy a vivacious sex life, dream big dreams both as individuals and as a couple, start a family, buy your first house, and settle into life. But the life you started with begins to disintegrate into death. Job and career demand more time away from each other, a child suffers a debilitating injury or disease, a sudden death occurs in one of the families, the stock market plunges and decimates your 401k, or a business venture collapses. Then, unthinkably and unpredictably, your partner has an affair leaving you and the kids for a "new love." That is yet another form of death—it came to let loose loathing over love, inject insurrection into your intimacy, and defile your deepest desire of devotion.

Death. Just death—as far as the eye can see—death in our physical, emotional, and spiritual spaces. So many types, all with varying degrees of visceral damage.

There are *many* more examples than merely the ones I wrote about above, so take a moment to interject any of your own experiences you have endured throughout your life. Any number of the details and effects of death which I stated above could, or already do, apply to you for sure. In light of such an overpowering foe, how does one cope with such devastating disaster?

Martin Luther, 16th Century monk and theologian, once said, "Every man must do two things alone; he must do his own believing and his own dying."

Once we step away from the one-dimensional concept of death to understand that death can appear in multiple different forms, we are able to take the first step toward what we *believe*, which will lead to the ability to do our own *dying* with patience, peace, and perseverance.

> **Death will come, but residency is only granted when we allow it to linger in our minds, hearts, and souls.**

Knowing that we cannot escape death means that trying to ignore it, run from it, or hide away from it only makes life that much harder for us and everyone else around us. When death appears, there is a crucial mind decision and heart attitude which we can choose to adopt and live by—shake hands with death, accept what it takes, then ready yourself for what awaits after it is finished, after you send it on its way. Did you catch that? After *you* send it on its way! Death will come, but residency is only granted when *we* allow it to linger in our minds, hearts, and souls.

Think back for a moment on everything lost, stolen, or destroyed throughout your survival in this existence here on earth. I believe in *every* case, there was new life to be found afterward, but when death appears, we must *choose* to shake hands or not. By choosing not to look death square in the eye and firmly shake hands, we provoke a serial killer to pursue us—

we invite the architect of tragedy to take residence in our very bones!

I have watched too many people plummet into depression, alcoholism, drug abuse, domestic abuse, violence, criminal activity, and even suicide following a tragedy in their lives. Tragedy is the playground where death and the devil play ruthlessly. Every time, *every time*, they arrive at a tragic scene only to pull from their pockets a lie which always has the same message—there is no hope, so give up on life. Then they press with evil reckless abandon their sole goal of making you believe that lie however they can.

My friend, the choice of life after death is yours and mine. I am not saying it is not a difficult choice—death and the devil are masters, making evil appear good and darkness appear as light as they inflict their deviant deceptions to cause destruction. Yet we can conquer them and find life again after *any* circumstance they force upon us or trick they perpetrate against us. We need only understand that after death has gone, new life *will* arrive!

> **We must endure the inevitable death which will come so that we can experience the inexorable life which will bring transformation in our life *after* death.**

It may not look like you expected it to look. It may not feel like you expected it to feel. It will never replace equally that which death took—which is most often the single snare that disables us from seeing clearly or taking a step forward.

We get trapped in *what* used to be, *who* was lost, and *why* it happened—a maze we all try to solve and have spent way more time in than we should. If we would but shake hands with death, then *LET GO*, the maze would magically move its walls, transforming turns that once arrived at dead ends into corridors that reveal the exit to a new landscape for life.

Remember my depiction of the wildfire back at the beginning of all this? How it ravages through the forest, bringing death and darkness, only to have life overpower the charcoal and ash a brief time later? This force is the power of life. Death will come, yes, but so will life after!

We must endure the inevitable death which will come so that we can experience the inexorable life which will bring transformation in our life *after* death. Restoration, redemption, and resurrection are just a few beautiful scenes that lie beyond the putrid veil of death!

I lost my job, but I found a new one that offers better pay, a better work environment, better work/life balance. There it is, death stole the last job, but *life* brought a different new fulfilling job or career.

I lost my devoted friend, but in time they returned—with explanation, apologies, and the invitation to begin anew. There it is; death killed the friendship with deceit, but *life* rebirthed regret into the restoration of a meaningful friendship.

I lost my marriage, but I learned to love again—maybe that means the repentance of my unfaithful ex and remarrying, or perhaps that means I find a new spouse. There it is; death destroyed my most intimate relationship, but *life* reformed the loss into a discovery of deeper love.

No Death, No Life

There are other ways to describe the job, friend, or marriage loss scenarios above with different contributing circumstances or other outcomes. Still, the point remains the same—I must *choose* life by getting *through* death.

When my son collapsed, with nearly everyone telling me he would likely not survive, I had to reckon with a choice confronting me. Imagine if, after seeing my son lying in the ER, lifeless, death convinces me that there is no hope in this tragedy. Imagine if, believing the lie, I disappeared later that night to end my own life because the pain of losing my firstborn son was too much to bear. I would have *missed* the incomprehensible miracle of resurrection over the next 11 days! More importantly, I would have let death laughingly loot my future and inflict immeasurable pain upon my family for the rest of their lives!

Death is hard. *Life* is glorious!

Yes, but Kevin, what would have happened if Mark died, you say? I hear you. Not everyone is granted a miracle or restoration out of a tragedy, as I experienced with my son. I lost my son for three days; it was a void I learned could never be filled by anything in this life but Mark, so I cannot imagine losing him until the afterlife. My heart breaks for every parent that has had to bury a child—it is, I believe, one of the greatest annihilations that death can wreak upon our human spirit. Nevertheless, it changes nothing regarding the decision to *choose* life after death.

That may sound unempathetic or harsh but believe me, it is quite the opposite! If Mark had died, my grief would have been lasting and likely one of the hardest things I ever had to face until my final breath. Yet, I would not believe that he was in the grip of death any longer but rather *alive* with God above. That does not take away the loss of a loved one not being amongst the living here on earth, I understand. But it does take away the *control* that death would try to oppress me with—by my choosing to believe there is life after death, both for the one I lost as well as myself!

Often I think about the conversations I would love to have with all my grandparents who have passed away. You remember me sharing earlier that my grandmother Willie Ann Schlaegel passed away on Friday, November 8th, 2019, just two days before my son collapsed. Let's just say it now—that takes the prize as the winner for the worst weekend *ever* in my life!

Getting the news of her passing at work, I had to excuse myself into a conference room for 15 minutes to mourn and collect my emotions. I used to call her "Hot Stuff" every time I saw her, which got her all flustered, but I knew she loved it. I shared so many good times with her over the years, and it hurt to know I would not be able to have conversations with my grandma anymore—but I do not honor anyone by choosing to let death *ruin* me with depression, guilt, or regret while I am yet *still alive*.

> **The deceit of despair comes when we let the difficulty of death seep into the levity of life.**

I have heard it said, "life is hard," by nearly everyone I have met, quite honestly repeating it myself far too many times over the years. At this point, I unreservedly beg to differ with all I have experienced in my years of living. *Death* is hard. *Life* is glorious! The deceit of despair comes when we let the difficulty of death seep into the levity of life.

Death and life are painted on the same canvas and blend into each other at times across the center line, as I visualized for you at the end of the last chapter. However, it is essential to distinguish that we *cannot* let death move beyond the God-intended blending balance at the center line to seep into and take over the entire life side of the canvas.

Now we arrive where choice meets canvas—dark splashes of death will spill over onto light colors of life at times, but we must not fail in *never* allowing death to mix itself into every corner of our life canvas. We cannot let the difficulty of death seep into the levity of life!

At the beginning of the chapter, I spoke about the path of life passing through a cave where death assaults and a secret truth awaits. Let us return there now.

When I made my way through the cave, enduring death in all its thievery and murderous ways with my son, I exhaustedly reached the end of that dark cavern to the discovery of a dimly lit door.

The door stood over 10 feet tall, made of massive thick weathered oak wood, rectangular at the bottom with a half-moon arc for a top, but without a handle or keyhole of any kind. Taking a step closer, I see that there are small cracks where the light shines as slivers from the other side, the only source of faint light that enables me to see the door.

Standing close enough now to see more detail, I notice a prominent saying engraved erratically into the rough wood near the top, which reads, "No Death, No Life" in mysterious simplicity. Still a bit afraid of what may be present on the other side of this door which appears unable to be opened, I lean my face cautiously toward the door and press my left eye as close as I can to one of the cracks to get a glimpse of what lies beyond the wooden wall. But just as my retina reaches the crack, the light overpowers my eye, making it impossible to see anything. I quickly pull back my head, blinking hard to recalibrate the cave's darkness.

What do I do now, I thought? I have come all this way, and I am so close to escaping now, it seems, yet there is no handle and no keyhole—I cannot see what is on the other side of this gateway, and there is no way to open it.

Standing defeatedly in front of this daunting door, I fell to my knees, closed my eyes, and listened in the silence. Soon, a faint voice took flight on a wind passing through the cave, whispering, "Choose your destiny!"

It blew into my ears and then rose over my head. I opened my eyes to follow the voice as it trailed up and away, only to see the phrase, "No Death, No Life," glowering down at me yet again from the top of the door.

I knew immediately I had a choice to make. Would I stay in that cave, hounded by dark death, or would I find a way to open the door to light life? I rose to my feet, inches away now, as I raised both hands to just below my shoulders and prepared to press them onto the door with whatever strength I had left. I closed my eyes again, slowly lifted my right foot, and began to step forward.

Just as I moved, my fingers barely brushing the jagged wood, the door creaked loudly and swung open wide! A blinding flash of light blasted my tightly shut eyes, and a rush of refreshing air reached my fatigued face.

No Death, No Life

Feeling these sensations, I instantly raised both hands over my head as if to surrender to whatever had opened that dense door so easily. Nervously, I pried one eye open to a squint, only to encounter a breathtaking scene of wonder. Sensing that I was no longer in danger, I lowered my arms and opened both eyes wide to take in this haven of healing and harmony, which was like nothing I had ever seen before.

I made it. I had arrived. Death had ravaged me there in that cave, so I was not sure I wanted to see what was on the other side of this door that rested in a place that required me to walk through such horror and pain. Yet I had endured the darkness. I had survived the dastardly deeds to the delight of a door designed for destiny—unlocked by faith and opened only by my conscious choice to move *towards* life after death.

That shrouded secret truth is allowing our mind, heart, and soul to reach past its physical form alone to embrace that death has the intrinsic purpose of enabling life in all its fullness. I finally discovered what it meant to know the secret and walk through that door hidden at the back of that cave—without death, one cannot be witness to the implausible miracle of resurrection!

CHAPTER XII
RISE TO ALIVE

Then one of the elders said to me, "Do not weep!
See, the Lion of the tribe of Judah, the Root of David,
has triumphed."

—Revelation 5:5

Jesus answered, "I am the way and the truth and the life.
No one comes to the Father except through me."

—John 14:6

Life was tough for seven weeks following when my son left the hospital. I was back to my telecom job of ten-to-eleven-hour workdays, and my wife was back in her retail job during the holiday season—which meant long and unusual hours for her with it being the busiest time of year for that industry. There *should* be a standard accommodation in life that allows for six weeks off with pay after any severe life trauma. We needed it, but that did *not* happen.

Our days after getting home from the hospital quickly became a monotony of survival. We went to work, fell into each other's arms and onto the couch when we got home, and ate dinner (thanks again to everyone who brought us meals those days after we got home). After that, with whatever energy we had left, we tried to deal with persistent fatigue and feelings that were still bucking like wild horses within us.

Given the remarkable outcome we had been witness to, I honestly thought that our bodies and minds would snap back unfettered, even though the journey had been ridiculously rough. That was wishful thinking at best. Post-Traumatic Stress Disorder (PTSD) took hold shortly after Thanksgiving—following a week of Mark recovering at home—which began to affect us in ways we had never experienced before.

During the day, images of what we had seen in the hospital or reactions from our pain would appear at very unwelcome times. I had to get up from my workstation, and Crystal would have to retreat to the back room of her store often multiple times a day to calm down and get straight, as grief would unexpectedly blast up from within, resulting in tear-laden hyperventilating outbursts.

Preparation for the aftermath of a trauma is rarely part of the process for all its participants.

I am 6'4" with a large stature, so when I felt that landslide of emotion coming, I had to move quickly because being inconspicuous is hard for a guy like me under normal circumstances, much less trying to battle uncontrollable body mutiny. We managed (most of the time) to keep those very per personal flareups secret from the public around us, but it was a consistent challenge for months.

Rise to Alive

During the night, our helpful REM (Rapid Eye Movement) cycle turned into its evil twin, *unhelpful* REM (Really Enraged Motion), and wreaked havoc upon our attempts to rest. Multiple times I violently thrashed as I slept or jerked straight up in bed in response to memories flashing through my mind, waking both myself and my poor wife with a dreadful shock.

If you have ever experienced that before, you know that once the adrenaline gland opens wide, it is akin to a dragon swooping down out of the clouds spitting scorching fire into your entire body—then there is no sleep for a *long* while after that!

Other nights, my wife would sob in her sleep as nightmares tormented her mind, waking me up as she convulsed and trembled. Almost every night for seven weeks, one or both of us would fall prey to PTSD.

Preparation for the aftermath of a trauma is rarely part of the process for all its participants. Trauma affects everyone differently depending on what degree you were directly involved in, so in fairness, it is hard to equip someone properly. Yet, looking back, I wish someone at the hospital had taken the time to inform all of us about the nature and potential severity of PTSD.

You do not have to *lose* someone to death to experience the full effects of PTSD. Trauma comes in various forms, so let this be a heads-up to you when you experience any trauma in the future; know what PTSD is and how it may affect you or anyone else involved.

Crystal and I were blessed to have great friends and family to talk to and process things with, so we did so regularly when our energy and emotional capacity allowed. Telling this incredible story in person locally and on the phone for weeks, with a focus on the happy ending of Mark surviving, helped us cope.

By early January, the heavy PTSD was starting to subside. It helped that Mark was improving radically every week—being able to see, hug, and kiss our very much alive son was phenomenal therapy!

One night (still in early January), I had a vision as I slept. It began with me looking down at myself from a far-off drone-like view. I was standing in the center of a large open field which was diffusely golden from the light of the sun and colorful with ankle-high wildflower clusters spread out all around me, expressing beautiful shades of red, pink, orange, yellow, blue, and purple.

To my back, there was a tall mountain where the light shone brighter than where I stood—inviting and majestic—a stout symbol of all the soaring successful experiences life could offer. In front of me was a low valley where darkness dimmed it blacker than where I stood—uninviting and menacing—a haunting symbol of all the dreadful defeating experiences life could offer.

Zooming into the right side of my face, I could see tears streaming down my cheek. My face was filling with fear and firmly fixed down onto the valley, my eyes desperately searching the horrific landscape below as if I were looking for something or someone.

Then off in the distance, I saw another human figure approaching from my left. As this figure got closer, I could see that it was Jesus. With His eyes set on me, He hurried to my side. Without speaking a word, He opened His arms as I collapsed into His chest. As He held me up from falling to the ground, I could feel His unwavering strength as He embraced me tightly while I wept in anguish.

Gently, after a good while, He placed His hands on my shoulders and stood me back to my feet. When He felt that I was firmly upright, He took His right hand, put it on my chin, then lifted my head from its prostrate position. He stared deep into my bloodshot watery eyes, then smiled with empathy as compassion covered His countenance.

Confidently He began to speak, saying, "Kevin, I want you to wait here and keep your eyes on me. Do not look away; I will be back soon, my friend."

He removed His hand from my face, turned to His left, and began to walk directly toward the valley. After about fifteen significant steps in the field, the terrain turned down steeply, and with each step, His figure began to fade, growing smaller and smaller to my eyes.

I had witnessed the attributes of that valley for quite some time before Jesus had arrived and seen it for what it was. It was a desolate wasteland with trees that bore branches that looked like broken bones, ground that emanated ghastly ashes of grief, air that smothered light with shadow, and demons that hunted in ghostly savagery.

It was terrifying, not a place someone should willingly wander into without presuming no ordinary human being would ever return from such. As Jesus descended, it struck me that I was staring at the valley of death. Upon this realization, I whispered under my breath, "Even though I walk through the valley of the shadow of death, I will fear no evil, for You are with me."

Saying those words aloud made me realize that I had not shared with Jesus what I had been searching for down in that valley before He joined me in that field. You see, I was searching for my son. Death had stolen him away from me, taking him to a place where I could not see him, reach him, or save him. I suddenly felt a mix of hope and fear at the same time as questions rushed from my heart to my head. Did Jesus know? Was He going to find my son? Was my son still alive, or was he dead?

Jesus was no stranger to me; I knew Him. I knew His story. I knew He had raised others from the dead during His time here on earth from reading my Bible. I knew that He died and was resurrected. But that was *His* story—a story that was thousands of years old, which I had not been directly witness to—so how could that help me here and now with what I was facing in my modern-day dilemma?

Standing nervously in the field, I moved forward a few steps closer to the valley as I watched Jesus move further and deeper. With my eyes affixed to Him walking a visible path through the wasteland, I began to see disturbing things.

Creature-like demons with repugnant red eyes, nasty scar-ravaged bodies, long razor claws, and blood-dripping teeth began lunging out from behind those twisted trees to swipe at this stranger who was now brazenly trespassing where all other living things fear to tread. Some just threatened, while others connected, drawing visible bodily reactions and blood spatters from Jesus' body. He did not stop to acknowledge them nor fight them—He merely took each hit and continued moving forward down through the revolting valley.

Marching on as the attacks continued, He was now extremely far away from where I stood. So small to my eyes now, I pushed my head forward, straining to see what was happening. He reached a small clearing and then stopped. I could see something vaguely on the ground to the left, there beneath His feet, but I dare not blink in fear that I may miss any detail of what He was doing.

With His back still to me, He decidedly raised His arms, stretching them out as far as possible to either side of His body with the fingers on His hands pointed toward the sky. Then, He circled one complete revolution right where He stood as if to command all the hellish creatures to cease their onslaught.

He lowered His hands as He turned to His left and then dropped to one knee, picking up what I now could faintly see: a body lying on the ground. Jesus bowed His head over the limp body for a brief time, as if to speak, then rose back to His feet. Now facing me, He paused only to turn His head from left to right to straight forward, then began walking defiantly up and out of that grisly gorge.

Clutching the body close to His chest, Jesus moved more swiftly now than He had when He walked in. His head was upright as He moved powerfully past all those creatures who were only allowed to stomp and snort their threats this time because they dare not touch this One who clearly ruled over them.

I grew impatient, moving to the edge of the field. Jesus was carrying a body, but I still could not see any signs of life. Though I knew Jesus was moving faster toward the field than when He had first walked away from me, it felt like a lifetime waiting for Him to clear the valley safely.

Climbing the last hill, with the threats silenced and the diabolical demons having returned to their dungeons, Jesus cleared the haze, and I saw His face, smiling once again. There in His arms was my son, with eyes open, alive, and looking now at me!

Overwhelmed, I fell to both knees amongst the wildflowers and began to weep openly. Finally, Jesus reached me, laid my son in my arms, then stood next to us with His hand resting upon my head as He looked toward heaven above while the view of myself and the whole scene faded backward as the vision ended.

Waking up after receiving a vision like this was intense! I was literally sweating and crying as I laid there in bed because it was *so real*. My wife woke and when I shared the vision with her, she joined me in my tears as we talked about what it meant.

It revealed that I, that everyone connected to this story, had been witness to a modern-day miracle—not because of medicine, luck, happenstance, or any other human derived explanation (or excuse) to avoid a simple truth—but because Jesus Christ has power *even over death itself*!

Do not get me wrong. I am not ignoring the CPR performed on my son by Sam or the resuscitating efforts of the incredible paramedic team. I am not disregarding the medicine and machines that managed Mark, the gifted skill and knowledge of the medical or surgical staff, or any other factors that definitively played a part in my son's survival.

I am saying, however, that all those things performed the same way with the same level of care and urgency can (and most times do) play out differently for other patients with stats similar to my son's stacked against them. While there in the CCU during our 7-day saga, we heard multiple flat lines of patients who did *not* survive in other rooms of the CCU wing, having to endure the anguish of wondering if the loss which was occurring just feet from us would find its way into Mark's room.

Rise to Alive

I sincerely believe Jesus saved my son from death—resurrecting him right before our very eyes. Mark was dead, not expected to survive, but a higher power determined this was not to be his end.

I often joke that as Mark was getting ready to pass through the glowing gates of heaven above, Jesus caught sight of him only to loudly declare his objection by yelling, "Oh no, no, no! You are *way* too loud and energetic, son, and I am not ready to deal with all that just yet, so you turn around and march *right back* where you came from, mister!" It makes me laugh to know that may have been exactly how it went down when he was in the presence of angels courting the afterlife during his coma.

In all seriousness, I believe Jesus brought him back—walking right into the valley of death to pick him up and carry him back into the beautiful fields of life. If you are familiar (even in the slightest) with the story of Jesus' death and resurrection, then you should be able to comprehend at least why I cannot see what happened with my son in just three days as any mere coincidence.

Yet, I know there are skeptics out there; perhaps that is you as you chose to read this book simply because you know my son, or me, or another person in our family. If so, there is something I must say to the heart of the skeptic; the one who struggles to believe in God at all, much less a God who intervenes directly in the lives of human beings in such a way as you have just read about in this story.

I feel your doubt, I have wrestled it many times before myself, and I understand that struggle all too well. God, are you there? If you are anything like me, my ability to believe in a loving God has been astoundingly challenged by persistent pain, iniquitous injustices, and humanistic hypocrisy.

If you have been betrayed, abused, or victimized by any person (or worse yet, a friend) claiming to "believe in God," as I have far too often throughout my life, then I understand your skepticism of God himself.

> **The ability to believe in a *loving* God is astoundingly challenged by persistent pain, iniquitous injustices, and humanistic hypocrisy.**

While I understand it, I *implore* you to grasp that humanity's representation of God, while noble in effort *most* of the time, will indelibly be inadequate to rightly represent the precise truth of God's intent, integrity, and infallibility.

When those who are supposed to love us, supposed to have answers to help us, supposed to lift us when we fall—when they fail us, or even worse, stomp on us while we are down, it becomes a visual that we often project onto God in our times of trouble.

Is God truly all-powerful? Is God remotely trustworthy? Is God honestly loving? These are all questions that went through my mind as I stared at the lifelessness of my son; they are questions you yourself have or will ask when you face any severe suffering. It is ok. In all honesty, it is ok! It is downright human to invoke such interrogations and look to other logic to inquire, explain, and cope.

Did not Abraham, David, Peter, Paul, and *all* the other so-called pillars of the Christian faith cry out to question God about pain, injustices, loss, and even death? Indeed, they did! There is a book that explicitly recounts their stories and emotions. Don't believe me? Pick up a Bible and read through the book of Psalms to soak in the wildly erratic praise *and* lament in that narrative from David and others.

> **The human condition that most greatly plagues the soul of all people is unbelief.**

It would seem all too easy to point to medicine, coincidence, technology, or other readily tangible answers for how one could survive such trauma as chronicled in the pages herein. So, let us come at this rationally (which is a troublesome concept for our culture at this point in history, but let us attempt it nonetheless).

How can one rectify crediting any of those things I just noted above when the experts themselves—the ones who actively embrace modern medicine, technology, surgery techniques, and biological philosophies—are shocked and declare a survival and recovery like my son's a miracle? That rationale transports us to a place where the science, the procedures, and the practical reasons are *not enough* to explain the entirety of an event in someone's life. Logically, that leads us to an outcome that there must be *more* at work, which defies typical sensibilities, scientific data, and human intellect.

Is it so hard to believe? Is it that difficult to attribute a higher power was at work in this story or others like it? Is it that unbelievable if the people who could be claiming notoriety for "healing their patient" instead acknowledge that the story in this instance involved statistics, data, and exhaustive experience that *directly contradicted* the outcome which occurred?

It is not difficult at all; it is, in all actuality, entirely rational, logical, and reasonable.

Yet, there are *still* doubters and diverters who *must* argue as they battle against what is blatant, omit that which is obvious, and cancel what is perfectly credible. But in favor of what? Do I favor men and women who are finite, frail, and faithless with *any* aspect of life? Or would I instead favor God, who is infinite, indestructible, and influential over *every* aspect of life?

> **We mistakenly remove our belief from what is uncomfortably unseen by our eyes, unheard by our ears, or untouched by our hands in favor of that which our senses can comfortably contain.**

A.W. Tozer, 20th Century American pastor, and author, once aptly stated, "Unbelief is actually perverted faith, for it puts its faith not in the living God, but in dying men."

Now that is a true tragedy—when we excuse ourselves from kinship with a king for fellowship with the fallen.

The human condition that most greatly plagues the soul of all people is unbelief. We mistakenly remove our belief from what is uncomfortably unseen by our eyes, unheard by our ears, or untouched by our hands in favor of that which our senses can comfortably contain.

To remain steadfast in what you believe when things are normal—that is, I am healthy, lucky, wealthy, and happy—is hard enough. On the other hand, what happens when our circumstances become a game of Jenga, which crashes to the ground all the once steady and in-place pieces of our belief system?

> **What we *do* when worries, fears, or anxieties develop within is what genuinely matters because actions are the product of our *true* beliefs.**

It is positively ordinary to have some level of worry, fear, or anxiety form inside us associated with having to directly face any trauma, much less a potentially terminal condition for ourselves or others. What we *do* when worries, fears, or anxieties develop within is what genuinely matters because actions are the product of our *true* beliefs.

Ouch, that statement stings even as I write it because I know that my worries, fears, and anxieties get the better of me sometimes, which results in actions that stray from the belief I desire to be steadfast throughout my entire being. Such is the nature of us all—we are all guilty of unbelief and actions which reflect our weaknesses at some point. Nonetheless, it need not *end* there!

Imagine with me for just a moment that your son, daughter, father, mother, brother, sister, or closest friend in the world was in that hospital bed, lifeless, with no hope on the horizon, according to the wisdom of humanity. To whom then would you align your beliefs?

It seems like such a cruel image to force on you—your own loved one in that near-death state—given all you just read about with the unimaginable pain and trauma my son and all of us went through. Yet, even so, I am doing just that. Why? Because little in life becomes palpably real until it happens to your own mind, heart, and soul. So, I will ask it again differently; in the face of death, with whom would you, with whom *do* you align your beliefs?

In this saga, I chose and will continue to choose the One, Jesus Christ—the creator of all life who holds dominion over death—because He was able to rise to alive!

I understand if you are still not convinced because of what death has already taken from you and your life. I will not try to convince you further of who Jesus was (and still is) on a factual or logical level, as there are plenty of apologetics resources to provide all the evidence required for such belief. Although, I highly recommend this undertaking if you seek absolute truth as you try to survive in this relative piranha bowl we exist in currently.

What I will do is pray for you. I will pray your mind is released from the torment of lies, your heart is healed of the memories which cause you pain, and your soul is freed from the fear of death in each of its forms. Above all, I will pray that one day you awaken to life after death here on this earth *before* being confronted with the inescapable afterlife.

An overabundance of white noise (aka "lies") in our media-connected world makes it increasingly difficult to hear the whispers of truth, so I beseech you to seek out silence so that you can accurately discern the various rhetoric which vies for your belief. Step out of your gruelingly busy world—slash away all the wicked webs which have woven a prison around you—to embrace a solitude within your soul. There, you will hear the forgotten sound of solace, the encouragement of epiphany, and the presence of peace.

Rise to Alive

There is ridiculous rhetoric rampant in our current culture that would have us erase history, abandon the past, and forget the stories of yesteryear. This rhetoric would also have us neglect the life, death, and resurrection of Jesus. For no other reasons than we were not physically present to witness it, that it happened thousands of years ago, and that we as humans are obsessed with control and would instead make ourselves God of our own life.

That same rhetoric would ask me, "Kevin, why would you want to write a book about what happened to your son? It was such a horrific ordeal that was so harrowing. Plus, it was years ago now, so why bother?"

The answer is simple—because I *never* want to forget the miracle of my son's story as long as I live—nor do I want *anyone* connected to my life to forget it either! The death and life which comprise this story are essential to how we view what happens to us and how we respond in kind.

Death and life are both there within us. Right now, keep a finger on this page as I want you to close the book and take a few long-focused moments to stare at all the details of the front cover—go ahead, I'll wait.

Welcome back. What did you see?

A single lion, one face, yet two distinct halves—one side dark, scarred, decaying, scary, and dead—the other side light, royal, lovely, reassuring, and living. But how can that be? Surely death and life cannot exist together, right? Ah, but they can, and *they do*!

I find it interesting that even the Bible uses a lion to depict both death and life. In 1 Peter (chapter 5, verse 8), the apostle gives a final warning in his letter near the end of the chapter, which states, "Be self-controlled and alert. Your enemy, the devil, prowls around like a lion looking for someone to devour." There it is, death and the devil synonymous, as I explained earlier, always stalking and set to kill, steal, and destroy everything they touch.

Conversely, in Genesis chapter 49 (verses 8–12), a language is poetically used by Jacob as he speaks to his son Judah of a lion as a king—a prophetic word to a lion of the tribe of Judah—which is the lineage of Jesus Christ. Within the *first* book of the Bible is a reference to this lion.

Furthermore, again in the *final* book of the Bible, Revelation (chapter 5, verse 5) highlights yet another reference to this lion stating, "See, the Lion of the tribe of Judah, the Root of David, has triumphed." First and last, author and finisher, beginning and end, creator of life and victor over death into the life thereafter—this is the Lion of the tribe of Judah. There it is, life and Jesus, synonymous with power over death, hope after despair, and love unfailing throughout eternity.

What else did you see on the front cover?

Lightning strikes down to a pile of bones; the final image after death has had its way, leaving only hole-filled remnants of a life that once was. But wait! Out of that skeleton graveyard, an angelic being emerges, in light and life, and ascends towards the star-filled heavens!

The next time tragedy and death wander into your life—I invite you to pick up this book to stare deep into the face of this intense lion on the front cover to see the true nature of a majestic creature who cannot escape death yet, has the power to *rise to alive*!

Rise to Alive

Death will strike us, hard and unexpectedly, throughout our lives repeatedly. Yet I say again that need *not* be the end of our story. There *is* life after death. But we must remain steadfast in the valley of death—to continue to crawl, claw, and climb our way through, up, and out.

I didn't, or rather I couldn't, understand the importance of this philosophy until death forced me to endure its vicious attack. It was intent on devouring my son, my belief, my trust, my very understanding of God and life itself. To see my son Mark rise again was a blessing beyond the conceited calculation or manipulated measures that any human being may foolishly attempt to force into this fable of faith that will live on forever.

One can never understand the meaning of a life saved without implicit knowledge of the journey through the valley of death.

In January 2020, Brian and Crystal dropped in on Mark after he went back to his retail job and began to live life fully again. Crystal snapped a picture and sent it to me via text while I was at work. When I opened it, I immediately felt a thud in my throat and had to dismiss myself to a conference room again.

Mark and Brian in January 2020.
Brothers to the end of this life and beyond.

The showy smile on Mark's face and the effort Brian was making not to laugh aloud right there in the store filled every part of my brain with a blast of bliss. My sons, these two brothers, would go on laughing at each other, making memories with each other, and being there for each other as best friends.

To see in my mind this picture, then place it right next to the first image of Mark lifeless in the ER, is a collage I will never forget. He was dead, yet now he is so alive! The words to the old hymn "Amazing Grace" were ringing loudly in my ears. My son was lost, but now he is found—a gift that every engaged, loving father or mother knows and fully embraces for its meaning and value.

People often ask, "Do you wish that terrible accident never happened to your son?" It would seem a reasonable question at first consideration. While a "yes" may be the expected answer, to the contrary, I emphatically respond, "not even for a moment!"

Yes, it was a painful experience, yet it was also a *providential* experience. So, regardless of the pain, I want to remember *all* that took place—because one can never understand the meaning of a life saved without implicit knowledge of the journey through the valley of death. One is incomplete without the other!

> **When the hope we hold is greater than the fear we hide, we ignite a torch to light the way through the valley of death to the discovery of illumination within our soul.**

Once we understand a thing holistically, like death, it becomes easier to understand its anthesis. To embrace that death can take forms other than merely the physical, we are empowered to shed our fear of death in favor of something far greater than ourselves and anything we may be facing. Even whatever (or whomever) we lose to death can be seen in a new light.

William Gurnall, the 17th Century English author, once wrote, "Let your hope of heaven master your fear of death." When the hope we hold is greater than the fear we hide, we ignite a torch to light the way through the valley of death to the discovery of illumination within our soul.

There is an attitude I must adopt, a creed I must conceive, a faith I must forge, an expectation I must engrave upon my soul—that no matter what I have been through, no matter what death has taken from me, I can rise to alive! To *find* life, I must *endure* death.

For my own sake, for the sake of every life connected to my own, I must *RISE TO ALIVE!*

May these words resonate to the furthest reaches of your essence as a human being. May the adoption of this mantra result in a restoration of your ruins, a reclamation of your relics, and a resurgence of your revival!

With the whole of my humanity and spirituality, I say again, one final time; without death, one cannot be witness to the implausible miracle of resurrection.

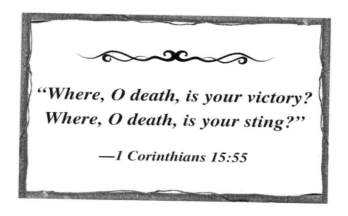

"Where, O death, is your victory?
Where, O death, is your sting?"

—1 Corinthians 15:55

NOTES

*All scripture references taken from *NIV Study Bible* (Grand Rapids, MI, Zondervan Publishing House, 1985).

Chapter I: Fateful Falling

1. This chapter epigraph is taken from C. S. Lewis, "Historicism," *Christian Reflections*, edited by Walter Hooper (Grand Rapids, MI: Eerdman's Publishing Company, 1967), p. 105.
2. Oswald Chambers, *The Complete Works of Oswald Chambers* (Discovery House Publishers, 2000).
3. John 14:6*.

Chapter II: A Fight with Death

1. This chapter epigraph is taken from J.R.R. Tolkien, *The Lord of the Rings*, (London, England, HarperCollins,1991).
2. P.O.D. ("Payable on Death"), American Band.
3. Lifehouse, "Flight*"* from the album *Out of the Wasteland* (Ironworks Music, 2015).

Chapter III: Awakening

1. This chapter epigraph is a quote from Martin Luther King, Jr., https://parade.com/252644/viannguyen/15-of-martin-luther-king-jr-s-most-inspiring-motivational-quotes/.

NOTES

Chapter IV: The Lion's Roar

1. Proverbs 30:30*.
2. *The Lion King.* Directed by Roger Allers & Rob Minkoff (Buena Vista Pictures, 1994).
3. Proverbs 28:1*.
4. Cat Tales Wildlife Center. Established 1991 - A 501(c)3 nonprofit organization. www.cattales.org.
5. C.S Lewis, *The Chronicles of Narnia Volume 2: The Lion, The Witch & The Wardrobe,* (Harper Collins, 1994).

Chapter V: Wrestling a Waking Gator

1. This chapter epigraph is a combination of two separate quotes from Jon Foreman, lead singer of the band Switchfoot, https://quotefancy.com/jon-foreman-quotes.

Chapter VI: War of Who & Why

1. This chapter epigraph is taken from A.W. Tozer, *Man, The Dwelling Place of God,* (Christian Publications, 1966).
2. Gary Chapman, *The Five Love Languages*, (Manjul Publishing House, 2001).
3. *The Lion King,* Directed by Roger Allers & Rob Minkoff (Buena Vista Pictures, 1994).
4. Tree 63, "Look What You've Done" from the album *Tree 63* (INPOP Records, 2000).
5. *Dumb and Dumber,* Directed by Bobby Farrelly and Peter Farrelly (New Line Cinema, 1994).

NOTES

Chapter VII: Monument of Miracle

1. This chapter epigraph is a quote from Saint Augustine, https://www.brainyquote.com/quotes/saint_augustine_1 48563.

Chapter VIII: Rough Ride to Weekend Wide

1. This chapter epigraph is a quote from Bono, Lead Singer of U2. https://www.goodreads.com/quotes/8199270-whenever-you-see-darkness-there-is-extraordinary-opportunity-for-the.
2. *The Hulk*. Comic book character created by Stan Lee and Jack Kirby. (1962).
3. Robert Louis Stevenson. *The Strange Case of Dr. Jekyll and Mr. Hyde*. (London New English Library, 1974).

Chapter IV: The Heart of it All

1. This chapter epigraph is taken from Oswald Chambers, *My Utmost for His Highest,* (Oswald Chambers Publications Association, 1963).
2. *The Lion King*, Directed by Roger Allers & Rob Minkoff (Buena Vista Pictures, 1994).
3. *Aquaman*. Comic book character created by Paul Norris and Mort Weisinger. (1943).
4. PSY, "Gangnam Style" from the album *Psy 6 (Six Rules), Part 1* (YG Entertainment, 2012)

NOTES

Chapter X: Surgery & Storybook

1. This chapter epigraph is taken from Tim Tebow, *Mission Possible*, (Colorado Springs, WaterBrook, 2022).
2. P.O.D., "Alive" from the album *Satellite* (Atlantic Records, 2001).

Chapter XI: No Death, No Life

1. This chapter epigraph is taken from a speech by Nelson Mandela, in Sophiatown, Johannesburg, in 1953, (Times Staff, Los Angeles Times, Dec 2013), https://www.latimes.com/world/worldnow/la-fg-wn-nelson-mandela-dies-famous-quotes-story.html.
2. Martin Luther, Quote https://www.goodreads.com/quotes/483947-every-man-must-do-two-things-alone-he-must-do.
3. William Tiptaft, Quote https://www.gracegems.org/book4/Tiptaft_treasures.htm.

Chapter XII: Rise to Alive

1. Revelation 5:5*.
2. John 14:6*.
3. Psalm 23:4*.
4. A.W. Tozer, *The Knowledge of the Holy,* (Harrisburg, PA, Christian Publications, 1961).
5. 1 Peter 5:8*.
6. Genesis 49:8 – 12*.
7. John Newton, "Amazing Grace". (1779)
8. William Gurnall, Quote https://www.brainyquote.com/quotes/william_gurnall_355092.
9. 1 Corinthians 15:55*

ABOUT THE AUTHOR...

Kevin Clayton is a follower of Jesus Christ, husband, father, son, brother, friend, writer, speaker, musician, producer, business professional, and humanitarian. He loves cooking, reading, photography, videography, listening to old and new vinyl records, and sightseeing in both modern and natural locations.

Kevin is happily married to his wife, Crystal Clayton, and they live in beautiful Coeur d'Alene, Idaho. Together, they enjoy playing card and board games, getting out in nature, spending time with family and friends, and vacationing on both the west and east U.S. coastlines.

RISE! Miracle Through a Father's Eyes is Kevin's first full-length published book. His next writing project is already underway, so stay tuned for more exciting releases in the future.